The Road to Rotterdam
Aston Villa FC Champions of Europe 1982
Rob Bishop

A
britespot
PUBLICATION

The Road to Rotterdam Aston Villa FC Champions of Europe 1982
A Britespot Publication

First Published in Great Britain by
Britespot Publishing Solutions Limited
Chester Road, Cradley Heath, West Midlands B64 6AB

October 2001

© Rob Bishop 2001

ISBN 0 9539 2887 X

Printed and bound in Great Britain by
Cradley Print Limited, Chester Road, Cradley Heath, West Midlands B64 6AB

Photographs kindly supplied by The Birmingham Post, Aston Villa FC and Popperfoto
No images may be reproduced in any format without prior permission from the above.

Design and layout © Britespot Publishing Solutions Limited

THE ROAD TO ROTTERDAM
ASTON VILLA F.C. CHAMPIONS OF EUROPE 1982

My name may appear on the cover, but numerous people have provided invaluable assistance in the production of this book.

For their help in various matters, I would like to thank Graham Hill, Alex Woolridge, Nadine Lawlor, John Williams, Bill Howell, Neil Cooper, Ian Findlay, Anna Burke, Mark Wilkes, Neil Rioch, Dave Woodhall, Richard Warburton and my lifelong pal Rob Johnson.

Thanks are also due to The Birmingham Post and Villa archivist Reg Thacker for access to their photograph libraries, to Pam and Dave Bridgewater for allowing me to raid their Villa "shrine" and to Villa receptionist Marie Priest, who succeeded where even UEFA were unable to help by providing a full list of substitutes for the European Cup-ties of 1981-82.

Most of all, though, I am indebted to the people who made it all happen. I wasn't covering Villa during the early eighties so I didn't attend any of the matches mentioned in these pages, but the players involved have taken me on an unforgettable journey.

Rob Bishop, 2001

For my daughter Helen, who was still sucking her thumb when all of this took place but who has acquired an insatiable appetite for Aston Villa.

VE Day

" All I could think about in the last few minutes was getting my hands on that trophy. When the final whistle went it was joy, joy, joy. Every time I watch the final on TV, I always find it a special moment when the cup is presented. I think: 'Yes, I've been there, done that.' It still gives me a magical feeling."

Dennis Mortimer's photographic memory provides a perfect snapshot of Aston Villa's delight at winning the European Cup on a humid night in Rotterdam in 1982 . It was undoubtedly the club's finest hour and Mortimer, as captain, had the honour of being presented with, and holding aloft, European football's premier prize.

For Mortimer, Villa's Victory in Europe Day also vindicated his team's League Championship triumph 12 months earlier, when everyone outside Birmingham had only grudgingly acknowledged their right to the title. Those critics who felt the 1981 English crown should have gone to Ipswich Town have been equally reluctant to dwell on Villa's European Cup triumph. For some reason, it remains an achievement which has never received the recognition it deserves.

This book, hopefully, will put the record straight - through the eyes of those people who created a wonderful piece of Aston Villa history. The players involved in that triumphant campaign have spoken frankly about their many experiences, both on and off the pitch, along the road to Rotterdam.

Peter Withe's 67th minute winning goal against Bayern Munich obviously provided the focal point of Villa's first venture into the European Cup, but by then the squad had already been through a whole range of emotions. They shivered together in Iceland, twice had a taste of Communism and endured a terrifying night of violence in Belgium before Withe's goal crowned a resilient final performance against the West German giants.

Villa's domestic form that season left a lot to be desired, and finishing 11th was hardly the hallmark of defending champions. But their adventures in foreign fields invariably brought the best out of them, possibly because they drew inspiration from the two other English clubs who had followed the same path so successfully in previous seasons. Liverpool had won the trophy in 1977 and 1978, followed by Nottingham Forest in 1979 and 1980, with the Merseysiders regaining it in 1981. Five years of English supremacy presented Villa with a hard act to follow, but they were equal to the task.

"We didn't play particularly well in the league that season," says Kenny Swain. "We were nowhere as good as the previous year, but as each European tie came along there was somehow a different focus about us. We were solid and so determined in those games, and we seemed to have a different mentality. We gave 100 per cent concentration and because of the success of the other English clubs we always felt we had a psychological advantage.

"There was an aura about English clubs in Europe at that time, almost a feeling of invincibility, and we carried that through with us. I'm not saying we felt invincible, but our opponents always seemed to go into the games with trepidation. I'm sure that was due to Forest. No-one on the Continent knew much about them when they first went in the European Cup but after they won it two years running there was bound to be respect for the English champions. Their success laid the foundations for us, and we felt we could tackle anybody."

Villa's self-belief became stronger with every round as they overcame teams with much greater European experience. Maybe no-one anticipated any real difficulty in beating the Icelandic part-timers of Valur in the opening round, but Dynamo Berlin, Dynamo Kiev, Anderlecht and Bayern Munich would all have fancied themselves to get the better of these upstarts from the English Midlands.

For their part, Villa were quite content to be regarded as underdogs from round two onwards, confident that their ability to operate as an effective unit would see them through against opponents who invariably boasted at least a couple of world class individuals.

"We were determined to show what we could do, and people started to take notice after we beat Berlin and Kiev," says Allan Evans. "But the important thing was that *we* believed and it didn't really matter what other people thought. We were a closely-knit unit. It wasn't that we went out socially all the time, but the work aspect was spot on and we knew each other's strengths and weaknesses. That was hard for outsiders to penetrate."

Gordon Cowans adds: "We had a great team spirit, which is what took us so far. We had good players and lots of ability, with everyone complementing each other, but the spirit was just as important. If you didn't pull your weight there would be three or four team-mates, usually senior players like Ken McNaught, Dennis Mortimer, Peter Withe and Des Bremner, telling you to get your finger out. There was no way you would be allowed to be out there on the pitch and not give everything you had. If anyone started slacking, he was soon told about it."

The sense of belonging also extended to the touchline. Throughout their nine-match campaign, Villa made substitutions on only three occasions, but that did not detract from the sense of importance of being given a watching brief. Nigel Spink, who made such a dramatic entrance to replace the injured Jimmy Rimmer after only nine minutes of the final, certainly welcomed the opportunity of being on first team duty in such prestigious matches.

"At that time there was only one substitute allowed in league games," he recalls. "The reserves usually played on Saturday afternoons, so I never felt part of what was going on with the first team. But that European campaign brought everyone together because we always had a squad of 16. It was the same for other people who were also on the fringe, like Andy Blair and David Geddis. They played the odd league game, but it was in the European ties that we all felt together."

Sitting on the sidelines was nothing new to Blair. Signed from Coventry City during the summer after Villa's Championship triumph, he spent a large proportion of his debut campaign in claret-and-blue waiting hopefully on the sidelines, although he actually started two of the European Cup games - the away legs against Valur and Dynamo Kiev - as well as making a two-minute appearance when Mortimer was injured in the home game against the Russians.

"I was substitute by myself in a lot of matches that season, so when we had five subs in the European games, I regarded myself as chairman of the bench!" he jokes. "We created our own camaraderie. Obviously we would have preferred to be playing but there was a great spirit among us and we were all happy to be involved in such a great adventure. I joined Sheffield Wednesday when I left Villa and their manager Howard Wilkinson had a great saying: 'It's amazing what can be achieved if no-one minds who takes the credit.' Maybe it didn't occur to us at the time, but that's how it was when Villa won the European Cup."

The passing of time, of course, has brought radical changes to the competition, which now bears little resemblance to its original format. Since 1992 it has been known as the Champions League rather than the Champions Cup, run in its early stages on a mini-league basis involving not just the champions of the participating nations but, in some cases, the runners-up and third-placed teams, as well. This obviously necessitates more football, and that, theoretically, makes it more difficult to emerge triumphant. But don't try telling that to Tony Morley, the winger whose trickery set up Withe's Rotterdam winner.

"People say it's harder to win the Champions League than it was to win the European Cup, but I don't agree," says Morley. "You can argue that we played only four two-leg ties to get to the final and there's obviously a lot more games involved now. But you can lose a couple of times in the qualifying stages and still go through. As far as I'm concerned, the competition doesn't really start until the quarter-finals, which is when one slip can mean you're out. It was like that for us in every match."

Peter Withe was certainly conscious of the precarious nature of the tournament's knockout element. A £500,000 record signing from Newcastle United in the summer of 1980, the burly striker had contributed 20 invaluable goals to Villa's title success in his debut campaign, giving him a second Championship medal to add to the one he had won with Forest in 1978. He was even more anxious, though, to make his mark in Europe, having missed out first time around.

"It wasn't just the final which was special for me," he insists. "I'd left Forest after they won the title and I thought I would never have another chance to play in the European Cup. But I was ambitious and eager for success, which is why I joined Villa. From the start of our run you could sense a hunger right through the side to go on and win it."

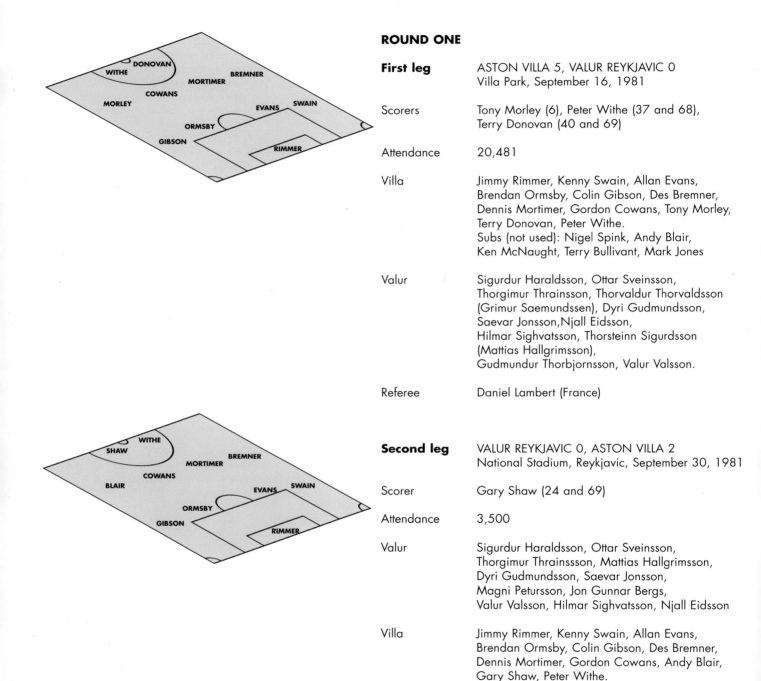

ROUND ONE

First leg

ASTON VILLA 5, VALUR REYKJAVIC 0
Villa Park, September 16, 1981

Scorers

Tony Morley (6), Peter Withe (37 and 68),
Terry Donovan (40 and 69)

Attendance

20,481

Villa

Jimmy Rimmer, Kenny Swain, Allan Evans,
Brendan Ormsby, Colin Gibson, Des Bremner,
Dennis Mortimer, Gordon Cowans, Tony Morley,
Terry Donovan, Peter Withe.
Subs (not used): Nigel Spink, Andy Blair,
Ken McNaught, Terry Bullivant, Mark Jones

Valur

Sigurdur Haraldsson, Ottar Sveinsson,
Thorgimur Thrainsson, Thorvaldur Thorvaldsson
(Grimur Saemundssen), Dyri Gudmundsson,
Saevar Jonsson, Njall Eidsson,
Hilmar Sighvatsson, Thorsteinn Sigurdsson
(Mattias Hallgrimsson),
Gudmundur Thorbjornsson, Valur Valsson.

Referee

Daniel Lambert (France)

Second leg

VALUR REYKJAVIC 0, ASTON VILLA 2
National Stadium, Reykjavic, September 30, 1981

Scorer

Gary Shaw (24 and 69)

Attendance

3,500

Valur

Sigurdur Haraldsson, Ottar Sveinsson,
Thorgimur Thrainssson, Mattias Hallgrimsson,
Dyri Gudmundsson, Saevar Jonsson,
Magni Petursson, Jon Gunnar Bergs,
Valur Valsson, Hilmar Sighvatsson, Njall Eidsson

Villa

Jimmy Rimmer, Kenny Swain, Allan Evans,
Brendan Ormsby, Colin Gibson, Des Bremner,
Dennis Mortimer, Gordon Cowans, Andy Blair,
Gary Shaw, Peter Withe.
Subs (not used): Nigel Spink, Tony Morley, Ivor Linton
Terry Donovan, Mark Jones

Over The Moon

T he aeroplane descended through the clouds, revealing a whole new world to its occupants. Aston Villa's players and officials were about to land in Iceland, but it felt like they were arriving on another planet.

As their chartered Icelandair Boeing 727 approached the United States Air Force base in Keflavik that Monday afternoon in late September, there were gasps of astonishment all around the cabin.

As far as the eye could see, the bleak terrain presented little more than black dust and volcanic rock, conjuring up images of a lunar landscape. Which is exactly how Gary Shaw recalls it. The Birmingham-born striker, fit again after the groin injury which had forced him to miss the first leg against Valur two weeks earlier, had been eagerly looking forward to the club's first European Cup excursion. The forthcoming game, though, was the last thing on his mind as he gazed out from the plane window.

"When we arrived in Iceland it was like landing on the moon," he remembers. "The place was covered in rocks and black dust, which was totally alien to us. I'd never seen anything like it."

There was little relief from the boulder-strewn landscape during the 45-minute drive from Keflavik to Reykjavik, although Iceland's capital city at least offered more familiar surroundings, not least at the club's base, the Hotel Saga. A well-appointed, modern hotel, the Saga boasted an impressive restaurant which offered excellent views of internal flights landing at the smaller Reykjavik Airport. Not that Villa's players were overly concerned about the local sights. They were too pre-occupied with trying to keep warm.

Monday and Tuesday were pleasant enough, littered with bright, sunny periods, but by Wednesday, they had given way to a gale blowing directly from the Arctic and the lunchtime temperature was a shivering 35 degrees fahrenheit. It didn't improve by kick-off time, either, as the wind-chill factor took hold.

On a tiny ground overlooked by mountains, Gary Shaw scored both goals in a 2-0 success which completed a comfortable 7-0 aggregate victory. If his memories of a largely uninspiring game have long since faded, however, he and his team-mates will never forget the conditions in which it was achieved.

"I've never been so cold on a football pitch," he says. "Most of us wore long sleeves and quite a few of us had T-shirts underneath, which was something we never normally did. Iceland is well known for woollen garments and I was given a jumper as a souvenir of our visit. I've never worn it since, but I was certainly grateful for it while I was there. The wind was strong too. One of my goals was a left-foot volley which I have to admit was wind-assisted as it flew past their 'keeper into the top corner. The guy simply never moved."

While Shaw and most of the team sensibly opted for long-sleeved shirts, defender Brendan Ormsby took it upon himself to defy the freezing conditions. "Throughout my career I never liked wearing long-sleeved shirts," he says. "Whenever I had to, I always rolled the sleeves up anyway, because I found them so restrictive. We had a choice in that game, so I wore short-sleeves - and I regretted it. It was ice cold. My arms were freezing and my hands were like blocks of ice. I was just relieved to get in the shower and thaw out, but it certainly took a long time."

'I was sitting next to Ivor Linton, and the gel in his hair started to freeze!'

At least the 11 players selected for the starting line-up could attempt to keep themselves warm by running around. There was no such relief for the five substitutes, one of whom, winger Tony Morley, was more than a little disappointed to find himself relegated by manager Ron Saunders to a touchline view of the action. Morley, after all, had scored Villa's opening goal in the first leg, and his trickery down the left wing made him a potential match-winner every time he went into action. His form had dipped in recent matches, however, and with Villa holding a 5-0 lead, Saunders clearly decided the former Preston and Burnley player's presence was not crucial on this occasion. "Ron was a manager who liked to keep people on their toes, and I was left on the bench," says Morley. "But there wasn't a dug-out, we were out in the open and I've never been so cold in my life. My feet were like blocks of ice. I was sitting next to Ivor Linton, and the gel in his hair started to freeze!"

LUNAR LANDSCAPE
The barren scenery which greeted Villa's players
and officials on their arrival in Iceland

Freezing temperatures were not the only inconvenience suffered by Villa that night. They also had to endure the pungent aroma which drifted across the tiny stadium from an adjacent fish factory. Defender Allan Evans recalls that one training session had to be curtailed because he and some of his colleagues were literally bending over and heaving as they struggled to contend with the dreadful smell which filled their nostrils.

It was no better come match-day, with Shaw claiming the stench wafting across the ground was so strong he could almost taste the fish and full-back Colin Gibson describing it as the most horrible smell he had ever experienced. It was no great surprise then, that the players were relieved just to get the game finished so they could turn their attentions to the homeward flight.

Despite the smell and a 40-mile-an-hour wind which blasted down the rutted and bumpy pitch, Saunders' side performed admirably in football's most northerly outpost. Having thwarted Valur's enthusiastic but limited attacks early in the match, Shaw opened the scoring on 24 minutes following skipper Dennis Mortimer's low free-kick and then produced the 20-yard volley which, by his own admission, owed a lot to the elements as it swirled and dipped just inside the post.

From that juncture, the visitors cruised in, with Shaw denied a hat-trick only by a goalline clearance. By the end, with a passage to the second round safely assured, even the fishy smell became bearable, and one player had hardly noticed it anyway. Andy Blair, signed that summer from Midland rivals Coventry City, had struggled to force his way into regular first team contention, but was grateful for the chance of making his European Cup debut in Iceland.

Blair is adamant: "I can't really say I took much notice of the smell from the factory because I was just happy to be playing. The prospect of European football was really appealing, and that had been the massive attraction of joining Villa from Coventry. As it turned out, I didn't get many games because they were such a good side but Ron Saunders put me in for the match in Iceland. Tony Morley told me 'You'd better take care of that shirt - you won't have it for very long.' I remember thinking: 'What an arrogant arsehole!'

"When he said it, I took it as a bit of an insult, but I have to say Morley was a very good player in that team, and I have the greatest respect for what he did for them. Saunders obviously used me to rile Morley. I was glad to have the chance of playing, but looking back I reckon my inclusion was the manager's way of giving out a message to the rest of the side that no-one could take his place for granted. You have to say it was good management."

Saunders also displayed his powerful managerial skills shortly after the party returned from their venture to the edge of the Arctic Circle, delivering an icy blast of his own. It had come to his attention that on the night Villa had arrived in Reykjavik, one group of players had stepped out of line by heading into town in search of entertainment.

Alcoholic beer is banned in Iceland, but there was no shortage of Champagne in the nightclub where the errant group gathered to mingle with the locals. The joviality soon died down, though, when secretary Steve Stride and the club's medical officer Dr David Targett walked into the establishment.

'We thought the game was going to be a cakewalk.'

"We thought the game was going to be a cakewalk, so there didn't seem much harm in going out for a drink." says Gary Shaw. "We were all having a good time when in walked David Targett and Stridey and we thought 'Oh,no, we're in trouble.' To be honest, I think they kept it to themselves, but the boss found out somehow and when we got back home he called us together for a meeting. He seemed to know certain players had been there, although I'm not sure he knew I was one of them. In the end we all owned up. I can't recall being fined, but Ron just wanted to make his point and let us know we couldn't get away with things like that."

Tony Morley and Gordon Cowans were also among the group who broke the curfew, and both players recall how the hugely popular "Doc" Targett, who died in 1997, actually joined in the illicit festivities.

"At one point we were doing the pogo dancing that punks were into at the time," says Morley. "The first inkling I had of Doc Targett being in the place was when he suddenly appeared on the dance floor and started doing it with us! He was that sort of guy, always looking to enjoy himself, and the lads thought the world of him. We had a great time, but we were given a right old dressing down afterwards."

Cowans' version of that Monday night out is more expansive. "We went out for a walk and ended up in a bar, having a couple of drinks," he explains. "It just went on from there and we were fooling around, which was out of order really. We had a feeling the tie was won, but it was still very unprofessional.

"That sort of thing went on more in those days, it was all part of the team spirit. When we were back home, a lot of the lads went out together. We shouldn't have done it over there, but it happened and luckily it didn't cost us anything. We were all on the floor and all of a sudden Doc Targett was bouncing around between us. We realised the chairman and the other directors were there too, so we made a swift exit after that. The directors didn't seem to mind, but the manager was absolutely furious when he found out. It must have been about a month later when he discovered what had happened. He sat us all down in the dressing room and asked who had gone out. Eventually we all owned up and he let us know in no uncertain terms that he wasn't happy."

The manager had also been unhappy on the day before the match. Although blissfully unaware of his players' indiscretion the previous night, he was not impressed when physio Jim Williams asked permission to go on an aerial tour of the island, which had been arranged for the Villa officials by their accommodating hosts.

Allan Evans takes up the story: "Our directors were invited on a sight-seeing flight in a small plane and Jim Williams wanted to go. Ron said it was okay as long as he was back in time for our training session that afternoon. When Jim didn't turn up Ron decided to play a trick on him, so we strapped up the legs of Mark Jones, one of our young reserves, to make it look as if he had suffered a fracture.

'Of course he's been drinking. It was the only way we could kill the pain!'

"Jim was outside the hotel waiting for us when we got back and his face was a picture when he saw some of the players carrying Mark. We had also poured brandy over Mark and when Jim smelled it, he was horrified. He asked if Mark had been drinking and was clearly in a state of panic. 'Of course he's been drinking,' Saunders snapped back at him. 'It was the only way we could kill the pain!'

"After we sat down and thought about it, I really felt for Jim, who was basically a nice guy who had just been a bit unfortunate. It was a cruel thing to do to him, but Ron Saunders had that ability to teach people a lesson. I don't think Jim ever missed another training session."

Another Williams, full-back Gary, also has vivid memories of the Valur game - and he wasn't even there. He and his fiancee Liz Williams had been due to be married on Sunday September 27, but had to postpone the wedding when the European draws were made and they realised he would have to travel to Iceland within 24 hours of the ceremony.

"In the end, it didn't matter because I was injured so I didn't travel," he says. "But I was glad we put the wedding back. I wanted the other players to be there and that would have been difficult if we'd stuck to the original date.

"Why we had picked the end of September in the first place, I haven't got a clue, but we eventually got married two weeks later." On Sunday, October 10, at St Paul's Church, Hamstead, Miss Elizabeth Williams became Mrs Gary Williams in a ceremony conducted, appropriately enough, by the Reverend Roger Williams. Gary's team-mates were there to witness the event, but had to report back for training the next morning as their newly-wed pal enjoyed two days off for the briefest of honeymoons.

If the first round of the European Cup disrupted a Villa wedding, it also coincided with a Villa birth. Des Bremner had been present when his twin sons Liam and Nial had been born a couple of years earlier, but was on his way to Iceland when his wife Pat went into labour with the couple's third child. Needless to say, Des was in regular telephone contact with home throughout the trip, learning on Tuesday September 29 that Pat had given birth to another son, Paul.

The birth of Aston Villa as a European Cup team two weeks earlier had gone smoothly, too, despite an initial administrative hiccup in the staging of the club's first match in the competition.

THEN THERE WERE THREE
Terry Donovan, standing in for the injured Gary Shaw, pounces from close range after Withe had headed down Kenny Swain's free-kick

THEN THERE WERE FOUR
Withe drives home left-footed at the far post following another fine Bremner cross

As secretary/director Steve Stride says in his 1997 book *Stride Inside The Villa*: "What do you do when you are trying to book accommodation for a party of 30 players and officials from a visiting club, and there isn't a hotel room to be found anywhere in Birmingham?"

The reason for the problem, Stride explains, is that an Autumn Fair was taking place at the National Exhibition Centre and every hotel, both in the city and its immediate boundaries, was fully booked throughout September. The diligent secretary spent hours trying to resolve what could have been a major embarrassment, finally coming up with the required rooms at the Post House in Stoke-on-Trent, 50 miles north of Birmingham. The Icelandic directors, thankfully, accepted the inconvenience without complaint, although Stride admits he told a white lie by suggesting the journey from the Potteries to Villa Park took around half an hour. As if to test his debatable theory, he was stopped for speeding at 90mph on the M6 as he returned from Valur's hotel, following the customary dinner for visiting officials the night before the match.

'I don't think many people regarded us as a threat.'

As for the game itself, Villa were stepping very much into uncharted territory. Valur had been national champions 17 times, but Iceland was hardly regarded as a major football stronghold, as the club's record outside their own back yard seemed to indicate. In 20 previous European ties, they had only managed one victory, beating Glentoran 1-0 in the European Cup of 1977-78, and even then they had gone out on aggregate. Nevertheless, Villa approached their debut in the competition with considerable caution. "Any time you start off in a cup competition, you're always happy to be drawn against one of the less fancied teams," says Dennis Mortimer. "Then again, we weren't fancied either. We had won the First Division, and the English champions had gone on to win the European Cup for the previous five seasons, but I don't think many people regarded us as a threat. The crowd (20,481) was disappointing, too. It made us wonder if our supporters really believed in us, or maybe they just felt the match wasn't attractive enough."

Attractive or not, Villa had no intention of becoming complacent. Tony Morley: "It was a case of Into the Unknown and we really had no idea what to expect. We thought we would be good enough to win, but there were a few nerves around the dressing room because we knew we were on a hiding to nothing. Even though Valur were part-timers, we knew a lot of top sides had come up against lesser opposition down the years and had found it far from easy. Ron Saunders drilled into us that we had to be professional." The message clearly got through. After just six minutes, Morley had the satisfaction of scoring the club's first European Cup goal when he drilled home a low shot from just outside the penalty area following Mortimer's short free-kick, and Villa showed no signs of easing off.

By half-time it was 3-0 as Peter Withe headed in Des Bremner's 37th minute cross and Terry Donovan pounced after Withe had headed down a Kenny Swain free-kick five minutes later. Goalkeeper Jimmy Rimmer, who had earlier dealt capably with a couple of speculative long-range efforts from the visitors, was subsequently not troubled during a second half which was even more one-sided than the first. Withe powered his way through to make it 4-0 in the 68th minute before Donovan outjumped the Valur defence to claim his second and Villa's fifth.

It was quite a night for the 23-year-old reserve striker, who had started the season playing for the reserves and was only in the team because of injuries to Gary Shaw and David Geddis. Not that there would have been any worries on Saunders' part about having to include the former Grimsby

THEN THERE WERE FIVE

Donovan gets on the end of Morley's deep centre to complete the scoring with a close range header

Town player, who had already hit the target three times in the opening weeks of the season, once against Sunderland and twice in a 3-1 win over Tottenham Hotspur.

Before the Valur tie, Donovan had boldly predicted "I'll back myself to score goals" and he was as good as his word. With a touch more composure, in fact, he would have marked his only European experience with a hat-trick. Both he and Withe were guilty of some bad misses and he fluffed an 80th minute chance when the goal was at his mercy. Even so, he helped to lay the foundations for Villa's triumph, and his contribution will never be erased from the record books.

Withe certainly has the greatest respect for Donovan's efforts in that opening tie. "It was one of the few occasions when Terry had an opportunity to come into the side," he says. "David Geddis usually deputised if myself or Gary Shaw had an injury. Terry was a strong player and we complemented each other very well in that match. He took his goals well, although I think we both came off the pitch feeling we should have scored hat-tricks."

Amazingly, Valur felt they still had a chance in the second leg. Ron Saunders went into the boardroom afterwards and one of their officials told him: "Just wait until we get you back to Iceland, we'll show you how we can really play." The manager relayed this piece of information to his players, but no-one seemed unduly concerned. Landing on the moon was going to be no problem.

BETTER LATE...
Gary and Liz Williams on their wedding day, surrounded by the full-back's team-mates. The big day
had been postponed for two weeks because the original date clashed with Villa's trip to Iceland

NEAT FINISH

Gary Shaw (No.8) gets in front of a defender to convert Dennis Mortimer's free kick after 24 minutes of the second leg

WIND-ASSISTED

Gordon Cowans collects the ball from the net after Shaw's long-range shot had flown past goalkeeper Haraldsson for Villa's second goal

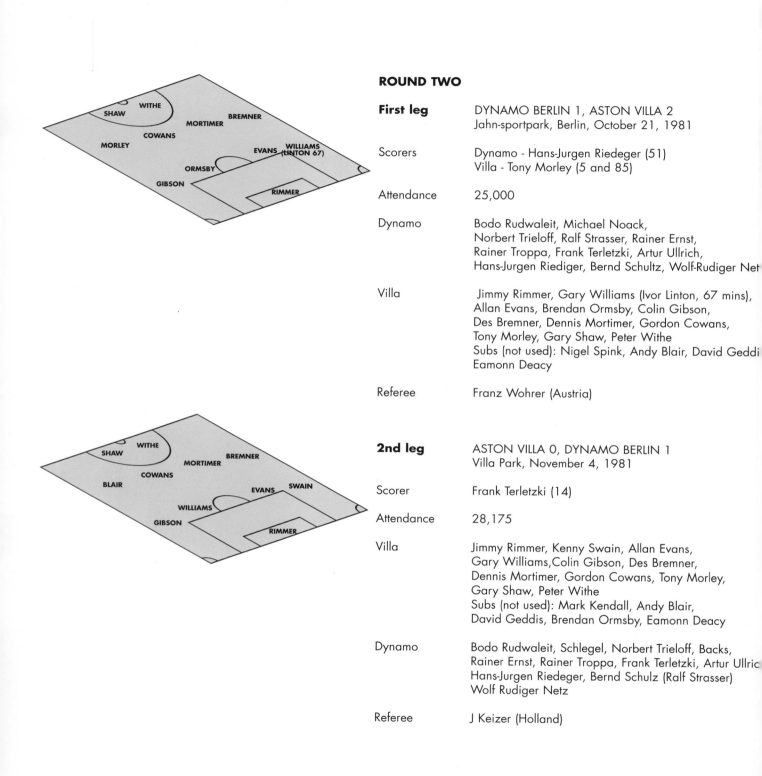

ROUND TWO

First leg	DYNAMO BERLIN 1, ASTON VILLA 2 Jahn-sportpark, Berlin, October 21, 1981
Scorers	Dynamo - Hans-Jurgen Riedeger (51) Villa - Tony Morley (5 and 85)
Attendance	25,000
Dynamo	Bodo Rudwaleit, Michael Noack, Norbert Trieloff, Ralf Strasser, Rainer Ernst, Rainer Troppa, Frank Terletzki, Artur Ullrich, Hans-Jurgen Riediger, Bernd Schultz, Wolf-Rudiger Net
Villa	Jimmy Rimmer, Gary Williams (Ivor Linton, 67 mins), Allan Evans, Brendan Ormsby, Colin Gibson, Des Bremner, Dennis Mortimer, Gordon Cowans, Tony Morley, Gary Shaw, Peter Withe Subs (not used): Nigel Spink, Andy Blair, David Geddi Eamonn Deacy
Referee	Franz Wohrer (Austria)
2nd leg	ASTON VILLA 0, DYNAMO BERLIN 1 Villa Park, November 4, 1981
Scorer	Frank Terletzki (14)
Attendance	28,175
Villa	Jimmy Rimmer, Kenny Swain, Allan Evans, Gary Williams, Colin Gibson, Des Bremner, Dennis Mortimer, Gordon Cowans, Tony Morley, Gary Shaw, Peter Withe Subs (not used): Mark Kendall, Andy Blair, David Geddis, Brendan Ormsby, Eamonn Deacy
Dynamo	Bodo Rudwaleit, Schlegel, Norbert Trieloff, Backs, Rainer Ernst, Rainer Troppa, Frank Terletzki, Artur Ullric Hans-Jurgen Riedeger, Bernd Schulz (Ralf Strasser) Wolf Rudiger Netz
Referee	J Keizer (Holland)

Backs to the Wall

He could hardly have made the dash more quickly had he been trying to escape to freedom a few yards away. Tony Morley, though, was not running in fear of a bullet in his back. He was the one in possession of the lethal weapon - a football, rather than a gun - and he was about to deliver a killer blow to Dynamo Berlin's European Cup hopes.

All the drama that damp October night unfolded on the Communist side of the infamous wall, rather than in the graveyard of no-man's land between east and west. Witnessed by a capacity crowd inside the Jahn-Sportpark Stadium, plus a few guards from the nearby Berlin Wall, Morley's exhilarating 90-yard run culminated with a piercing shot which effectively ensured Aston Villa's passage to the quarter-finals.

Villa, in turn, would fall victim to an East German sniper called Frank Terletzki in the return match two weeks later, but Morley's deadly double strike on foreign soil would ensure they went through by virtue of the away goals rule. Both his goals in Berlin counted double after an absorbing second round tie finished 2-2 on aggregate, but it was his second, five minutes from time which is always remembered more vividly.

There had been nothing wrong with his first, a stunning volley with the game just five minutes old. But his 85th minute winner, after Dynamo had equalised and then missed a penalty, was of such breathtaking quality that it was subsequently voted Goal of the Season by the Midland Soccer Writers.

It was certainly difficult to argue with the journalists' choice, and Peter Withe is happy to endorse it. "Tony had scored the Goal of the Season in our Championship campaign with a tremendous run and shot at Everton," Withe recalls. "But his second goal in Berlin was even better."

Morley started his run from Villa's penalty spot as Withe, back helping an under-siege defence, headed clear a left-wing corner. As the ball bounced over Gary Shaw - who had also dropped back to relieve Berlin's intense pressure - Morley took it in his stride, neatly skipped away from a lunging challenge and embarked on the loneliest run of his life.

Even with desperate opponents bearing down on him, he maintained both speed and composure before firing low past the diving frame of 6ft 7in goalkeeper Bodo Rudwaleit from just inside the penalty area. You are never likely to see a more clinical piece of finishing, but if the flying winger was outwardly calm, his mind was in turmoil.

"It seemed a long, long way because the pitch was very heavy," he says. "My run took me past a couple of players and left me with only the goalkeeper to beat but suddenly there was time to think and I usually foul up in situations like that. This time, thankfully, I got it right. The 'keeper had come out to close down the angle and I knew I couldn't chip him because he was so tall. There wasn't much to aim at, so I decided to hit it low and close to his body, and it went in."

'Those were the best two goals I've ever seen. And by the way, I'm fining you a week's wages!'

Morley's reaction to scoring was strange to say the least. Initially a picture of delight, his mood seemed to change in a flash as he turned towards Villa's bench and stuck two fingers up to manager Ron Saunders. It most certainly wasn't a Victory-sign, for it transpired that player and boss had exchanged words on the training pitch the previous day.

"I'd had a bit of a go with Ron," Morley recalls. "I was trying a few things and he said: 'You'll never score two goals in a match because you're too flash.' So after I scored my second, I ran past the dug-out and stuck two fingers up to him. I was just trying to tell him I'd scored twice - at least, that's the story I'm sticking to! He didn't say a word to me after the game, or for about a week afterwards. Then he called me into his office and said: 'Those were the best two goals I've ever seen. And by the way, I'm fining you a week's wages!' At least he gave it to charity."

Morley's winning goal lit up the murky night for Villa's travelling band of supporters among a capacity crowd largely populated with soldiers, but it had hardly been the brightest of trips. This, don't forget, was seven years before West and East Germany were re-united, and the Communist sector of Berlin was dismal in the extreme, leaving the visitor with images of greyness, poverty and lightbulbs which seemed to generate no more than 30 watts. As Morley recalls: "It was grim and depressing in East Berlin. I went to one of their top stores and everything was dirty. The stadium was near the Berlin Wall and when we were training we could hear the guard dogs barking in the distance."

Gary Shaw also has memories of the menacing dogs which, he says, created an eerie backdrop to that pre-match training session, although the tense atmosphere and drab surroundings came as no surprise to skipper Dennis Mortimer and defender Brendan Ormsby. "I described it as the dreaded trip behind the Iron Curtain," says Mortimer. "I'd been to that part of the world once before, going to Czechoslovakia with Coventry City in the old Inter Cities Fairs Cup, so I was aware we would have poor conditions, a poor hotel and a lot of red tape to get into the country. Needless to say, the East Germans didn't disappoint us. It was everything I had expected."

Ormsby agrees, even if his second visit was slightly more relaxed than his first: "I'd been to Berlin before, with England schoolboys, and an East German army officer had taken great delight in telling us how they shot anyone who tried to escape to the west across the Wall. I can't recall anything like that when I went with Villa, but it was still a depressing place, and the match was played on a cold, damp night."

At least Villa's party were afforded a comfortable, if not exactly luxurious stay at the 37-storey Hotel Stadt Berlin, the tallest building in the city, while their officials were treated to a touch of culture in the form of excursions to Hitler's Bunker and the Brandenburg Gate. Secretary Steve Stride also received an unexpected visit at the hotel from three British corporals, stationed in West Berlin, who were desperate for tickets. The army officers had to hang around for six hours while

STRIDE EARNS HIS STRIPES
Secretary Steve Stride is at ease before paying attention to the business of organising tickets for three corporals who had travelled from West Berlin for the game

Stride negotiated with Dynamo officials and awaited a reply, but their long wait was rewarded when the trusty secretary came up with the tickets they were seeking.

Their short trip across the city certainly proved worthwhile, Villa producing what was arguably the outstanding performance of the tournament, a feat which was all the more commendable given their problems in defence. Gary Williams, normally a left-back, switched to the right to deputise for Kenny Swain, who was ruled out by an ankle injury - and Williams, in turn, was forced out of the action when he took an early knock on his knee and eventually made way for the inexperienced Ivor Linton.

Villa's opponents, whose correct title is Berliner Football Club Dynamo, had been East German champions for the previous three seasons, but the match had only been in progress for five minutes when Ron Saunders' side stunned them with a classic goal on the counter attack.

Accepting Allan Evans' pass just inside the Berlin half, Shaw launched a flowing move with a smart turn before releasing the ball into Mortimer's path. The skipper played it wide to Des Bremner, who chipped a teasing cross into the home goalmouth. Shaw, having continued his run, missed out in the aerial challenge, but as the ball dropped just inside the penalty area, Morley arrived perfectly to send an unstoppable volley past Rudwaleit and into the bottom corner.

The visitors held their advantage until the 51st minute, when the man they most feared, East German international striker Hans-Jurgen Riedeger, pounced with a downward far post header from Ralf Strasser's free-kick - and the situation looked certain to deteriorate further when Dynamo were awarded a controversial 80th minute penalty following Linton's challenge on Wolf-Rudiger Netz. It seemed to be a perfectly fair sliding tackle by the youngster, who actually came away with the ball, but Austrian referee Franz Wohrer immediately pointed straight to the spot.

'When Jimmy kept out the rebound, I felt we had one hand on the cup.'

What followed was sheer drama and was undoubtedly the crucial action of the whole campaign. Artur Ullrich sent goalkeeper Jimmy Rimmer the wrong way from the spot with a calm side foot shot, only for the ball to come back off the left-hand post. Even then, a goal looked inevitable as the rebound hit Rimmer's foot and rolled back into Ullrich's path, but the German midfielder was unable to get any power behind a left-foot effort which hit the recovering Rimmer's left leg and looped over the bar.

Villa's relief was immense, and it was, Morley contends, the moment he was convinced they were heading for Euro glory. "I'm a great believer in fate," he admits. "When Jimmy kept out the rebound, I felt we had one hand on the cup, even though it was only the second round." Five minutes later, Morley brought his own gut feeling nearer to reality with the scintillating run which secured the unlikeliest of victories, one from which Villa's players derived enormous satisfaction.

"The lasting impression of the Berlin team is their athleticism," says Dennis Mortimer. "Pace and strength were big factors in their game, but they also had a lot of ability. They were very strong and were good runners with the ball, so we had to be on our toes. But we went about it in the right way - defending in depth and then looking to hit them on the break. Tony's second goal was a classic counter-attack.

DIVING IN VAIN
Goalkeeper Bodo Rudwaleit is unable to keep out Tony Morley's fifth-minute volley, much to the
delight of Gary Shaw (left)

"Berlin's penalty was a dodgy decision by a European referee who didn't see the game the same as us. Every time you lifted your foot six inches off the floor, it was a foul, which was very frustrating. I felt we were playing against an inconsistent referee and linesmen, but we came through it."

Gary Shaw was equally delighted. "Berlin were a good side, full of super, technical players," he says. "We were under a lot of pressure, but Jimmy Rimmer had a blinder and we just played on the break. Tony scored two great goals. I vividly recall the second because I misjudged the flight of the ball, but I dragged one of their players with me and we both missed it. It bounced over us and fell to Tony, who ran from deep in his own half and produced a great finish. We were really under the cosh at times but it was a fantastic result."

'It was almost unreal to have the guards watching from the Berlin Wall.'

While Morley and Rimmer were the night's heroes, Allan Evans and Brendan Ormsby also emerged with a lot of credit for the way in which they shackled Riedeger. Apart from his goal, the normally lethal East German marksman was afforded very little space, and frequently drifted to the wing in an attempt to find a way through.

That made life busier for left-back Colin Gibson, who recalls: "I ended up marking Riedeger. He was supposed to be a striker, but he kept wondering out to the right to try and put pressure on me. He kept drifting wide but I think I handled him okay and I came off the pitch thinking I'd done a sound job. We must have seen a lot of each other because we swapped shirts at the end.

"Dynamo were no mugs, but we gave a great team performance and it was a superb win in strange circumstances. It was almost unreal to have the guards watching from the Berlin Wall. Going from West Germany to East Germany wasn't just like going into a different country - it was a different world altogether."

Victory behind The Wall was, as Gordon Cowans put it, "a massive result", but Saunders and his men had seen enough from their opponents to know the tie was far from over - and two weeks later the events of the final 10 minutes in Berlin assumed even greater significance.

The manager again made a defensive switch, although it was unforced this time. Swain, having quickly recovered from his injury, had returned to the side for the intervening First Division matches, but Saunders decided to play the fit-again Williams in central defence in place of Ormsby, whose form had been disappointing since the first leg. Fourteen minutes into the game, the Villa boss must have questioned his own decision as his team were opened up down the right by Riedeger and Bernd Schulz for skipper Terletski to drive low past Rimmer and bring the tie level on aggregate. Dynamo had once again proved they were perfectly capable of scoring, and they had a further 76 minutes in which to grab the goal which would take them through to the competition's last eight.

As it turned out, the threat of a second from the visitors was evident only in a nail-biting 15 minutes, after the boys in claret-and-blue had crafted a succession of chances which were denied either by the giant Rudwaleit or some amazing goal line clearances which had Peter Withe and Gordon Cowans shaking their heads in disbelief. Had Villa been able to capitalise on their inventive

BREAKING DOWN THE WALL
Tony Morley hits Villa's winner past Rudwaleit after running the length of the pitch

approach work, the issue would have been settled by half-time, but as the game wore on, home nerves inevitably surfaced.

With nothing to lose, Dynamo suddenly pressed forward, Riedeger unleashing a close range drive which thudded against a post and across the face of goal before Rimmer once again saved the day with his feet, just as he had in the first leg. He kept out Riedeger's low shot with his right leg just as the Midlanders appeared to be facing elimination, and his team-mates will remain eternally grateful.

"We were living dangerously at the end," admits Gary Shaw. "Jimmy made a great save and Berlin hit the post. If either of those had gone in, it would have been curtains for us. That's how close we were to going out."

It had certainly been a tense, delicately-balanced contest, and one which made a mockery of so-called home advantage. "I felt we played a lot better away from home in that tie," says skipper Mortimer. "There was a theory about Iron Country teams not travelling well, but that wasn't the case with Dynamo Berlin. After they scored, we really had to be on our guard. We knew we would be out if they got a second goal. When the final whistle blew, it was something of an anti-climax. We had gone through, but we had lost the game, so it didn't seem right to be celebrating. But it was a great feeling to have reached the quarter-finals, and looking through the teams left in, it wasn't exactly a Who's Who of European football.

"There was no AC Milan, Barcelona or Real Madrid, although Liverpool and Bayern Munich looked dangerous. But there is no such thing as an easy game at that stage of the European Cup - and we ended up having to go back behind the Iron Curtain."

The quarter-finals also threw up a piece of European cup history. Although English teams had won the competition for the previous five years, this was the first time two teams from these shores had reached the last eight. A betting man would surely have fancied holders Liverpool to progress against CSKA Sofia of Bulgaria, rather than Aston Villa to beat Dynamo Kiev of the USSR. Football, of course, has never been that simple...

SHAW-FOOTED
Gary Shaw fires a shot at goal during the home leg against Dynamo Berlin

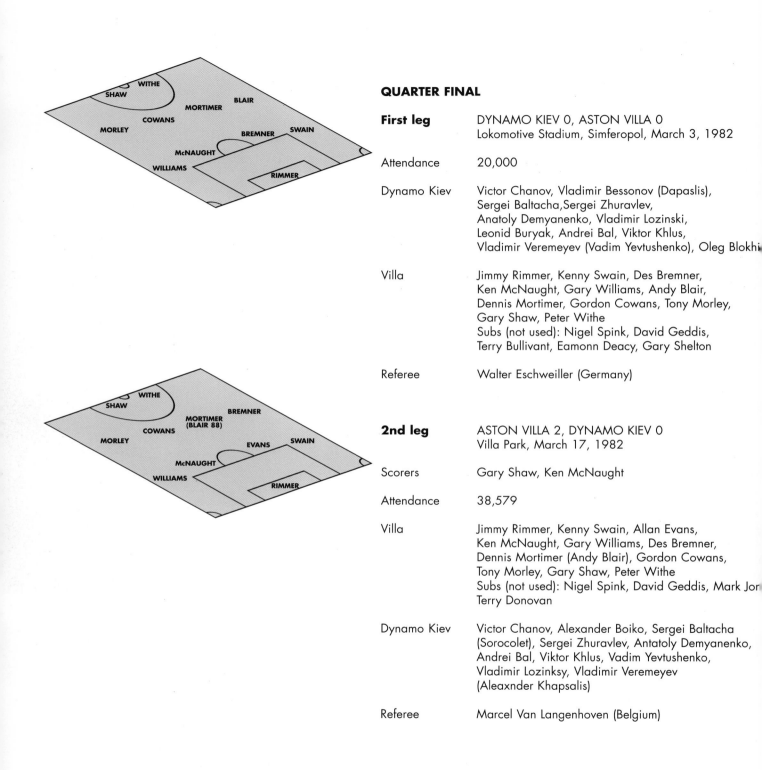

QUARTER FINAL

First leg   DYNAMO KIEV 0, ASTON VILLA 0
Lokomotive Stadium, Simferopol, March 3, 1982

Attendance   20,000

Dynamo Kiev   Victor Chanov, Vladimir Bessonov (Dapaslis),
Sergei Baltacha,Sergei Zhuravlev,
Anatoly Demyanenko, Vladimir Lozinski,
Leonid Buryak, Andrei Bal, Viktor Khlus,
Vladimir Veremeyev (Vadim Yevtushenko), Oleg Blokhi

Villa   Jimmy Rimmer, Kenny Swain, Des Bremner,
Ken McNaught, Gary Williams, Andy Blair,
Dennis Mortimer, Gordon Cowans, Tony Morley,
Gary Shaw, Peter Withe
Subs (not used): Nigel Spink, David Geddis,
Terry Bullivant, Eamonn Deacy, Gary Shelton

Referee   Walter Eschweiller (Germany)

2nd leg   ASTON VILLA 2, DYNAMO KIEV 0
Villa Park, March 17, 1982

Scorers   Gary Shaw, Ken McNaught

Attendance   38,579

Villa   Jimmy Rimmer, Kenny Swain, Allan Evans,
Ken McNaught, Gary Williams, Des Bremner,
Dennis Mortimer (Andy Blair), Gordon Cowans,
Tony Morley, Gary Shaw, Peter Withe
Subs (not used): Nigel Spink, David Geddis, Mark Jon
Terry Donovan

Dynamo Kiev   Victor Chanov, Alexander Boiko, Sergei Baltacha
(Sorocolet), Sergei Zhuravlev, Antatoly Demyanenko,
Andrei Bal, Viktor Khlus, Vadim Yevtushenko,
Vladimir Lozinksy, Vladimir Veremeyev
(Aleaxnder Khapsalis)

Referee   Marcel Van Langenhoven (Belgium)

Russian Roulette

No-one was holding a gun to their heads, but Villa were left in no doubt that they were involved in a game of Russian Roulette as they prepared for their quarter-final clash against Soviet champions Dynamo Kiev. Between the draw in Zurich on December 11 and the first leg on March 3, Villa endured 12 weeks of uncertainty as their opponents engaged in the sort of cloak-and-dagger tactics usually employed by Russian politicians. Berlin had been drab and depressing, but the club's second trip behind the Iron Curtain turned into the ultimate football nightmare.

By mid-February, Villa had already encountered one trauma, manager Ron Saunders having resigned after a row with chairman Ron Bendall over funds for new players. While that upheaval had been eased by his assistant Tony Barton's smooth transition into a caretaker role, however, there were plenty of other headaches looming. More than two months after the European Cup draw, the club were not even sure where the away leg would be played. All they knew was that it would not take place in Kiev, where freezing conditions at that time of year invariably rendered the pitch unplayable.

That much was acceptable, and was actually more to Dynamo's disadvantage than Villa's. History showed, in fact, that Western European teams regularly fared better at this stage of the competition than their counterparts in the Eastern Bloc, where adverse weather meant that most countries were taking an enforced winter break. Indeed, similar freezing conditions had proved costly for Kiev in the quarter-finals nine years earlier, when they had been forced to play Real Madrid in Odessa. A goalless draw on "home" soil had been followed by a 3-0 mauling in the Spanish capital.

If the Russians could do nothing about the weather, however, their attitude to finding an alternative ground was hardly conducive to harmonious east-west relations. A deputation of Dynamo spies, arriving in Birmingham on January 30 to watch Villa's home match against Liverpool that afternoon, calmly explained that unreliable weather prospects meant it might even be the day before the quarter-final before the venue was established. That was clearly out of the question because the Russian Embassy was unable to grant the necessary visas until the venue had been confirmed. Secretary Steve Stride was then informed by telephone that the game might take place in the Ukranian capital after all - but that Tashkent on the Chinese border or Sevastopol on the Black Sea were two other possibilities.

At that juncture, Villa's patience snapped and their subsequent complaint to UEFA was followed by a February 19 directive from European football's governing body that the Dynamo club must confirm a venue within four days. The deadline was duly met, even if Villa were little wiser for finally knowing where they would be playing. The tie was to be staged in a place called Simferopol, capital of the Crimea, 300 miles south of Kiev. It was a name which meant nothing down Witton way, but at least preparations for the 2,000-mile journey into unknown territory could finally be set in motion.

Given the Soviet Union's dubious reputation for hygiene, Villa would probably have taken their own food even if they had been travelling to Kiev. The fact that they were heading for such a far-flung outpost made the provisions imperative and when their Aeroflot 160-seater jet took off from Birmingham on the first day of March, the players and officials were accompanied by 150 steaks, 12 dozen eggs and 112 pounds of potatoes, plus bread, cereals, coffee and tea. It was perhaps just as well, given the shortage of food in Russia at that time, even if Villa's culinary caution would initially be rendered a futile exercise.

The signs were ominous almost as soon as the plane had landed at the third attempt after coming down through dense cloud. Still feeling queasy from that harrowing experience, the visiting contingent were further sickened when they were informed that not only had their accommodation been switched but that the kick-off time was also being brought forward from 7pm local time to 5pm to suit television requirements.

'I expected to hear a Russian accent. I couldn't believe it when I realised he was a Scouser!'

Even the intervention of the mystery man who had accompanied the party on their four-hour flight failed to bring any joy at that stage, even if he would later prove to be the life and soul of the party. Not that Villa's players had noticed him before touching down on Russian soil. Kenny Swain, who hails from Birkenhead on the south side of the River Mersey, will never forget his introduction to the stranger in the Cossack hat.

"We were standing in the airport, milling around for half an hour or so, and getting very agitated," Swain recalls. "I noticed a guy, wearing a big black hat, who seemed to be representing us. He was chatting to the Kiev officials and then returning to Steve Stride and the Villa directors. I became inquisitive about what was going on, so I edged over to them, expecting to hear a Russian accent. I couldn't believe it when I realised he was a Scouser!

"I asked him what a Scouser was doing in Russia and he replied: 'The same as you - earning a living!' He then introduced himself as George Scanlon, head of the languages department at Liverpool Polytechnic, and told me he was there as our interpreter. I certainly hadn't noticed him on the flight, but it turned out he had been out to Russia in the past to translate for other English clubs."

Even so, Scanlon was powerless to do anything about the unforeseen change of hotel. Written assurances had been given that Villa would be staying at luxurious accommodation at the Black Sea resort of Yalta, but it transpired that Dynamo were staying there, and the English contingent were taken instead to the sub-standard Hotel Moscow in the muddy, industrial, unwelcoming town of Simferopol. Manager Barton, needless to say, was not impressed with an establishment which

NOT EXACTLY THE RITZ
The Hotel Moscow, which Des Bremner claims was not worthy of a one-star rating

most certainly did not offer the sort of comforts Villa had expected, and neither were his players. Des Bremner reckons the hotel, which had sparse furnishing, rock-hard beds and was barely worthy of a one-star rating, was not even up to the standard of a Salvation Army hostel, while Dennis Mortimer offers the opinion that the beds were "like something you would expect in an army barracks - wrought iron frames with spring bottoms and thin mattresses."

"The toilets left a lot to be desired, too," the skipper adds. "The seats weren't attached to the WC and we joked that we would have to carry them around with us in case someone went into our rooms and nicked them!"

Peter Withe would have been a prime candidate for toilet seat theft - because he had great difficulty in getting into his own bathroom. "When I first tried to open the door, it banged against something and I couldn't figure out what it was," he says. "When I got in there I realised the toilet was right behind the door, and I swear there was a plate on the back saying it had been made in 1901. When you ran water in the wash basin, it came out all shades of green and yellow, and I also ended up removing a couple of tiles from the floor. My feet were sweaty and sticky and as I lifted them, the tiles just came away."

The small beds were of particular concern to taller players like Ken McNaught who, despite his 6ft 2in frame, insists he has the ability to sleep anywhere and was not unduly bothered about his legs protruding over the bottom end. "But the bath was a problem," McNaught adds. "It was only a half-sized one, about three feet long, and all you could do was sit in the thing. It was impossible to get fully submerged. If you wanted to soak the top half of your body, it meant having your legs hanging over the edge. I don't know how some of today's superstars would have coped! The fact that the match was moved from Kiev probably helped us more than it helped them because they lost a lot of their home support, but the change of hotel and kick-off time were obviously intended to put us on edge. The Russians were very good at screwing things up for you and making life as difficult as possible. It wasn't the most salubrious of places."

'I didn't mind the dead bed bugs, but I objected to the whole family coming to the funeral!'

Gary Shaw agrees: "They messed us around a lot. Some of the lads took photographs of the hotel rooms. There were no curtains at the windows, it was difficult to get hot water and the hotel staff insisted on giving us early-morning calls we hadn't asked for. The noise outside during the night was pretty bad, too. They did everything they could to put us off."

At least club photographer Terry Weir helped to keep the players' spirits up. Famous at Villa Park down the years for his endless supply of wine gums and sharp wit, Weir walked into his spartan bedroom and declared: "It looks like I've already been burgled!" At breakfast the next morning, he again had the assembled gathering in fits of laughter when he quipped: "I didn't mind the dead bed bugs, but I objected to all the family coming to the funeral!"

It was the second day before Villa were able to savour some of the goodies they had taken with them. They had arrived late the previous night, and there had been no time to unload the skips carrying their various foodstuffs, so the hotel provided a snack of chicken soup and bread. Tony Morley's claim that there were feathers in the soup is possibly a little exaggerated, but the foreign body discovered by Gordon Cowans most definitely wasn't a figment of the imagination. He broke open his bread roll and stared in horror as a dead cockroach dropped out!

BEST SEAT IN THE HOUSE?
A glimpse of the dreadful bathroom
conditions Villa endured in Simferopol

"It was a big, horrible thing which looked as if it had been there for an eternity," Cowans recalls. "I lost my appetite at that point and when the other lads saw what had happened, no-one seemed very hungry any longer. The dining room was desperate, anyway - it was basic beyond belief - and most of us decided we could wait until the next morning, when we could get at our own food." Villa's steaks duly appeared on the Tuesday and, to be fair, there were certainly no complaints about the manner in which they were cooked. It seemed, though, that, the hotel management had imposed some form of rationing. Ken McNaught: "When our meals arrived, we couldn't believe

'The chef had cut each steak into three pieces.
Someone had to go and tell him we were actually
allowed a whole one each!'

it. The chef had cut each steak into three pieces, and someone had to go and tell him we were actually allowed a whole one each! The guy must have thought we were really greedy, but it just showed how food was in such short supply over there. When we left, there were a few steaks left over, so we gave them to the chef. He was over the moon because it meant he could feed his family for the next three months!"

Villa found Simferopol just as depressing as East Berlin had been, perhaps even more so because it was in the middle of nowhere and everything was dimly lit. There was also the constant imposing presence of KGB officers, with no-one really sure whether these stern-faced gentlemen were there to provide protection or ensure that their visitors from the decadent West did not step out of line. When the players did venture out, they settled for a stroll around the shops, although it hardly constituted window-shopping because of the scarcity of goods on view.

"Apart from training sessions, no-one went too far from the hotel," says Gary Williams. "But on the Tuesday afternoon we were taken to see a few of the local sights and we went to a huge department store. It wasn't like the smart stores we have in this country - it was like a jumble sale. There were piles of clothes on what looked like wallpaper pasting boards, and shoes scattered all over the floor. I also remember people queuing for everything. It was a 15 minute drive from our hotel to the training ground and every time we made the trip we were amazed by the queues outside all the shops. The poverty we saw really made you appreciate what you had back home."

The training facilities in Simferopol also left a lot to be desired, but to their credit, Villa had no intention of allowing their adversity to deflect them from the task for which they had arrived in this uninviting corner of the USSR. They would have to go about their business, however, without the services of key defender Allan Evans, who had injured his shoulder the previous Saturday when landing awkwardly following a reckless challenge from Coventry City's Garry Thompson.

"It had been a nasty game and myself and Garry had really battered each other," says Evans. "He tackled me almost neck high and I went over his leg and landed on my left shoulder. I felt it pop out and straight back in again. Garry was sent off for the tackle and our physio Jim Williams strapped my arm up. I tried to carry on, but five minutes later I had to go off and I had my arm in a sling over the weekend.

"I even had some treatment during the flight to Simferopol, but it didn't really help. We had a training session on the Tuesday but I couldn't join in very much and then I had the fitness test on the Wednesday morning to see how my shoulder was responding. I kept hoping against hope it would be okay but there was never any chance of me making it, which was a massive disappointment because I played in every other match."

MINGLING WITH THE MILITIA
Villa supporters in buoyant mood before the match against Dynamo Kiev. The Russian soldiers
seem bemused by it all

Evans' injury meant a reshuffle which created a new-look central defence, with Bremner dropping back to partner McNaught, who had missed the first two rounds with a knee injury. Andy Blair, meanwhile, took over on the right of midfield. It was a promotion which delighted Blair, and vindicated his decision not to move to pastures new even before he had completed his first season in claret-and-blue.

Blair explains: "I'd had a chance to go to Vancouver Whitecaps a short while earlier, but I turned it down because we were in the quarter-finals of the European Cup. That was too good a thing to give up, even though I had spent most of my time on the subs' bench. I'm a naturally pessimistic person, but I genuinely felt we had a chance of winning it. I was desperate to play first team football, and the North American League was at its height so it would have been a marvellous opportunity. But I wanted the European thing."

'I think he understood what I was saying. Most of it was accompanied by the word 'off.'

Even though Blair had not been a first team regular, he was entrusted with the toughest possible assignment on Russian soil - man-marking Kiev's Oleg Blokhin, a former European Footballer of the Year and the player who posed the greatest threat to Villa's chances of reaching the semi-finals. Within minutes of kick-off at the Lokomotive Stadium in Pushkin Street, Blokhin had underlined his menace with a penetrating run and a shot which struck the post, but the former Coventry City player stuck doggedly to his task.

"I felt I did a good job on Blokhin," he says. "He hit the post early on but apart from that I kept him reasonably quiet and I felt I played my part in the team plan. I kept talking to Blokhin to put him off his game. He may not speak English, but I think he understood what I was saying. Most of it was accompanied by the word 'off'! For me, it was a great experience to pit my wits against one of the best players in Europe, although I can't imagine Blokhin will remember playing against Andy Blair."

The game, played against a backdrop of a quietly appreciative but largely unenthusiastic crowd and the strange sight of Soviet soldiers perched on stools all around the touchline, was far from a classic. After Blokhin's early effort against the woodwork, Blair's persistence and some resolute defending by McNaught and Bremner ensured that Kiev's star player did not have another clear-cut chance and although substitute Vadim Yevtuschenko forced the ball into Villa's net near the end, the effort was disallowed. It wasn't clear whether the linesman's flag was raised for offside or a push on Bremner, but either way, the visitors were certainly not arguing.

Despite Kiev's greater pressure, Villa performed admirably to force an excellent goalless draw, which might easily have been transformed into victory. Morley's stinging first half drive was superbly pushed away for a corner by goalkeeper Victor Chanov, while Shaw had a glorious chance after the interval. "I missed a sitter," the striker readily admits. "Tony Morley made a great run and pulled it back to me at the near post. I flicked at it and I thought it was enough to beat the 'keeper, but he got a touch to it and it went just wide of the far post."

Several of Shaw's team-mates also felt he should have scored, but there were no complaints about the outcome. With a highly satisfactory result under their belts, Villa were able to relax for the first time since landing on Soviet soil, even if they were unable to follow their normal procedure of returning home straight after the match. A night-time reduction in Russian air traffic control seemed likely to cause delays which could have meant the party being stuck at the airport for five hours or more, so the decision had already been taken to fly back the following morning.

WIDE OF THE MARK
Gary Shaw misses Villa's best chance in Simferopol as his miscued shot is pushed away by
goalkeeper Victor Chanov

In the meantime, the pressure was off and it was time to party, with intrepid interpreter George Scanlon taking centre stage at a post-match function organised by Dynamo and the Ukraine FA. "George was a great character," says Shaw. "He could match the Russians drink for drink when it came to vodka. At the banquet after the game, he took over and started dictating when there should be a toast. Once he got going, we seemed to be raising our glasses every five minutes. It was hilarious."

The aroma of western decadence also filled the air, thanks to Small Heath MP Denis Howell, the former Sports Minister, who was an avid Villa supporter. "Denis used to enjoy a cigar," recalls Des Bremner. "After the game, he handed out a few to the lads back at the hotel. It wasn't totally new to us. Ron Saunders sometimes used to come around the bus with cigars if we had won an away game - although he never gave one to the younger lads."

'When I woke up, I was covered from head to toe in toothpaste.'

Inevitably, there was a price to pay for the indulgences which followed two-and-a-half days of frugal existence. Gary Williams, for instance, woke up with rather more than a thick head, having fallen victim of a practical joke by his team-mates. "There was a nightclub at the hotel and everyone was drinking pink Champagne," he says. "I had too much and had to be carried back to my room. When I woke up the following morning I was covered from head to toe in toothpaste and glitter had been sprinkled on it! I couldn't get it off, and I still had some glitter on my face when we got to the airport. For about a week afterwards, it was still coming off in the shower. They must have used about six tubes of toothpaste."

Such frivolity was soon forgotten. When Dynamo arrived in Birmingham 12 days later in readiness for the second leg, the Cold War resumed, and once again the match venue was very much at the heart of the controversy. The ravages of a severe English winter had left Villa Park in a dreadful state, and the central area of the pitch for the Midland derby against Wolverhampton Wanderers the previous Saturday had resembled a squelchy bog of turf and sand in which the players' boots had frequently become submerged.

Having had to surrender home advantage in the first leg, Kiev were certainly in no mood for the game to go ahead in such poor conditions, and at one point there was a genuine danger that it would either have to be postponed or switched to another ground. Fortunately, the heavy rain and storms which had lashed the pitch over the weekend gradually subsided, with groundsman Tony Eden and his staff working around the clock to ensure that the game could go ahead. The conditions, however, were far from perfect. Allan Evans, who returned to the side after recovering from his shoulder injury, recalls: "The pitch was battered. It was brown rather than green."

The playing surface may have left a lot to be desired, but the second leg against Kiev undoubtedly ranks among the great European nights at Villa Park. Barton's men had not been playing particularly well in the league, while their visitors were regarded as one of the favourites for the European Cup, but Villa's victory that night was far more emphatic than the 2-0 scoreline might indicate.

The atmosphere generated by the crowd of nearly 39,000 was electric, too, as David Geddis recalls from first-hand experience: "I was on the bench for most of the European games but the one that really sticks in my mind is the Kiev game, when I wasn't in the squad. I watched from

GOAL COMING UP
Gary Shaw is about to unleash a low angled shot which flashed inside the near post to put Villa
ahead in the second leg

the stand that night and the crowd were undoubtedly more intense than in any other home tie. The atmosphere was brilliant, and you sensed that people were starting to believe we could win the European Cup."

Villa's cause, in fairness, was also helped by an almost defeatist attitude by their opponents. Although Berlin's win in the Midlands had disproved the theory that teams from Eastern Europe do not travel well, the Russians were clearly unhappy about having to venture beyond the great gates of Kiev.

"The Russians weren't happy at all," says Gary Shaw. "They kept complaining about the state of the pitch, and they clearly didn't want the game played. Once they went 2-0 down we knew we had them, because their heads went down and they just weren't interested. I remember their coach Valeri Lobonovsky. He was sour faced, with never a change to his expression. He just kept moaning to the linesmen about the pitch."

Having squandered an inviting chance in Simferopol, Shaw was both relieved and delighted to make the breakthrough after just four minutes and 15 seconds of the return match. Ironically, though, he wasn't as sure of scoring as he had been with the shot which Chanov had pushed aside in the first leg. "I collected the ball after we had made an attack down the left and drove it hard and low. It was a tight angle and I thought the 'keeper would save it, but it squeezed between the post and his right leg."

Three minutes before half-time, a passport to the semi-finals was all but rubber stamped, McNaught using his height to good effect as he climbed at the far post to nod in a Cowans' corner. "That goal killed them off," says the central defender. "Everybody was aware of Blokhin's threat and he had shown glimpses of what he could do in the first leg. But after my goal went in, he wasn't really up for it, and we knew we had a great chance of making the semi-finals. My night was complete when Jock Stein came up to me after the match and told me not to book any summer holidays because I was in his thoughts for Scotland's World Cup squad. Unfortunately it didn't happen, but it was a nice feeling at the time."

While McNaught savoured the sweet tastes of his goal, Villa's victory and the possibility of a summer trip to Spain, his skipper endured a post-match experience to forget. It was bad enough when Dennis Mortimer went down injured two minutes from time and had to be substituted by Andy Blair, but that was only the start of the midfielder's problems. "I went for a one-two on the edge of the penalty area and as I moved for the return pass, I caught one of their players and went down," Mortimer recalls. "Normally you put your arms out to protect your fall, but for some reason my arm had got twisted and instead of my fingers going down first, it was the back of my hand. The momentum snapped my arm and I thought I'd broken it. I was in agony.

'By then the crowd were leaving the ground and the traffic was horrendous.'

"Doc Targett came on and strapped my arm up and put it in a sling. Doc decided I should go to hospital and we went to his car, but by then the crowd were leaving the ground and the traffic was horrendous. It took nearly an hour and a half to get there and I was in so much pain that it seemed like a lifetime. It would have been quicker to walk! Luckily the arm wasn't broken, although there was some damage to the ligaments. I missed the next few games in the league, but at least I was back in time for the semi-final."

HEADING FOR THE SEMI-FINAL
Ken McNaught climbs above Kiev goalkeeper Victor Chanov to score the goal which sealed
a 2-0 aggregate victory

Victory over a side containing half a dozen members of the Russian World Cup squad offered ample evidence that Villa's desire to become kings of Europe was more than a mere whim, even if their relationships with the Dynamo club had been somewhat strained. Yet Tony Morley admits he had a lot of sympathy for the strict discipline imposed on their quarter-final opponents.

"I felt sorry for Kiev's players when they came to Birmingham," he says. "Their hotel was obviously much more luxurious they they were used to, but they clearly weren't here to enjoy themselves. There was no sight-seeing or shopping. When they weren't training they had to stay in the hotel, probably in case they were tempted to defect!

"The coach driver who ferried them around while they were here told me he went to their hotel on one occasion to pick them up for training. He put the radio on so they could have some music to relax to - and one of their officials immediately turned it off again. You wouldn't have believed they were the same team who had given us such a hard time in the first leg. It was as if they didn't feel they had a chance without a lead, and they just didn't seem to have the heart for it. I went on to their bus after the match to wish them all the best, but there was no response."

THE PAIN GAME

Skipper Dennis Mortimer is accompanied by club doctor David Targett after injuring his arm in
the closing minutes. Little did Mortimer know he was heading for a traffic jam...

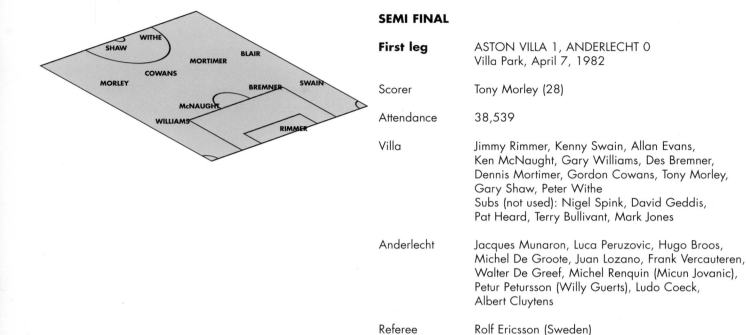

SEMI FINAL

First leg	ASTON VILLA 1, ANDERLECHT 0 Villa Park, April 7, 1982
Scorer	Tony Morley (28)
Attendance	38,539
Villa	Jimmy Rimmer, Kenny Swain, Allan Evans, Ken McNaught, Gary Williams, Des Bremner, Dennis Mortimer, Gordon Cowans, Tony Morley, Gary Shaw, Peter Withe Subs (not used): Nigel Spink, David Geddis, Pat Heard, Terry Bullivant, Mark Jones
Anderlecht	Jacques Munaron, Luca Peruzovic, Hugo Broos, Michel De Groote, Juan Lozano, Frank Vercauteren, Walter De Greef, Michel Renquin (Micun Jovanic), Petur Petursson (Willy Guerts), Ludo Coeck, Albert Cluytens
Referee	Rolf Ericsson (Sweden)

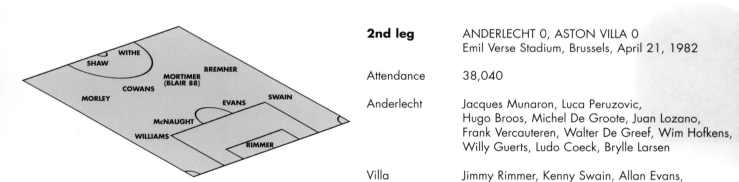

2nd leg	ANDERLECHT 0, ASTON VILLA 0 Emil Verse Stadium, Brussels, April 21, 1982
Attendance	38,040
Anderlecht	Jacques Munaron, Luca Peruzovic, Hugo Broos, Michel De Groote, Juan Lozano, Frank Vercauteren, Walter De Greef, Wim Hofkens, Willy Guerts, Ludo Coeck, Brylle Larsen
Villa	Jimmy Rimmer, Kenny Swain, Allan Evans, Ken McNaught, Gary Williams, Des Bremner, Dennis Mortimer, Gordon Cowans, Tony Morley, Gary Shaw, Peter Withe Subs (not used): Nigel Spink, Andy Blair, David Gedd Pat Heard, Mark Jones
Referee	Dusan Krchnak (Czechoslovakia)

The Battle of Brussels

Their march to the European Cup semi-finals had been conducted with almost military precision, so it was ironic that Villa's carefully-laid strategy should suddenly be unhinged by a member of Her Majesty's armed forces. They had become accustomed to crowds heavily populated with soldiers during their trips to East Berlin and the Soviet Union, but little could they have imagined that their hopes of Euro-glory would be jeopardised just across the Channel by a moment of madness involving an off-duty British soldier.

Football hooliganism was at its height in 1982, both in this country and on the Continent, and a night of violence in Brussels reached its climax during the second leg of Villa's semi-final against Anderlecht. As the Belgian champions launched a first half attack which ended with a shot over Jimmy Rimmer's bar, the mayhem which had already engulfed the Emil Verse stadium exploded into total confusion.

Even before the shot was fired, a spectator sporting a claret polo shirt had appeared in the goalmouth, lying down in the six-yard box before he was dragged away by half-a-dozen policemen.

It later emerged that the intruder from behind the goal was a member of the Sherwood Foresters, who had taken time off from his duties in West Germany to attend the match. His excuse for running on to the pitch was plausible enough, the lad claiming he had been trying to get away from the fighting which was raging on the terraces. That, though, was no consolation to Villa when Anderlecht subsequently cited his unwelcome intervention as a basis for appealing for the game to be re-staged.

An ugly flashpoint on an even uglier night resulted in the game being held up for six minutes and meant a considerably longer wait while UEFA officials debated the big question. Should Villa's 1-0 aggregate victory stand or should their opponents be granted a second opportunity of reaching the final? Anderlecht even called for Tony Barton's team to be expelled from the competition, and while that was never a realistic threat, Villa nevertheless had to endure an agonising wait to see if they would have to go through the second leg all over again.

Although they had performed admirably to emerge worthy winners over 180 minutes of football, there was a serious fear that their efforts might be rendered worthless by the deliberations of UEFA's disciplinary committee. Yet it really came as no great surprise to Villa's officials that the match was marred by such trouble. Club

secretary Steve Stride had been filled with trepidation from the moment he made his customary pre-match visit to check out the opposition's facilities and security arrangements.

Despite Anderlecht's standing as one of Europe's leading clubs, their precautions against crowd problems were virtually non-existent. With two jaunts into Eastern Europe behind them, Villa had experienced their fair share of Red Tape but they could never have anticipated that it would crop up in a different guise in Brussels. Stride was horrified to discover that the Belgian champions method of segregating supporters was, quite literally, a piece of red tape.

He described this flimsy, futile precaution against outbreaks of violence as "pathetic" and as events on the night of the match would conclusively prove, it was hopelessly inadequate. Running battles between English and Belgian fans resulted in 88 arrests and 18 people, including three policemen, needed hospital treatment for their injuries.

If Stride's worst fears were confirmed on that night of shame, the players also had more than an inkling that they were about to enter a battleground. Gary Shaw, who had watched Villa from

'...their shields shining in the reflection of the floodlights.'

the Holte End as a youngster, was acutely aware that major trouble was brewing. "As we pulled up to the ground I knew something wasn't right," he says. "I could always sense the atmosphere because I had been a supporter, and I could tell it was going to be bad. People were banging on our coach and it was obvious there was a lot of ill-feeling around. It was very hostile and we were just glad to get off the coach and into the dressing room."

Gary Williams agrees: "It was a hostile atmosphere. Their supporters were chucking beer cans and other objects at the bus as we arrived at the stadium, which was pretty intimidating. We wondered what we were going into. There had been no such problems in Berlin or Russia and it was surprising that it should happen in Belgium."

Shaw and Williams insist the trouble did not affect them but some of the more experienced members of the side admit they were distracted by the events which unfolded off the pitch. "It was quite a sight to see the riot police behind the goal, with their shields shining in the reflection of the floodlights" says Ken McNaught. "When I looked closer I could see that around 25 per cent of them were women, and Jimmy Rimmer noticed, too. He shouted to me: 'Have you seen this lot behind the goal?' "

Allan Evans' mind was in even greater turmoil, to the point where he actually attempted to do something about the increasingly worrying situation. He recalls: "I even tried to shout to our fans to calm down a bit. It was wrong of me because I should have been concentrating on what I was doing. But every time we had a goal-kick, my gaze wandered to the terraces. It wasn't very professional, but English fans already had a terrible reputation and I was worried about the consequences of what was going on. Whenever the ball was at the other end, I just kept looking anxiously towards the fans behind our goal. Anything could have happened, particularly when the guy ran on the pitch."

Several players went across to check out what was happening, Peter Withe making the point quite forcibly that the intruder was putting at risk the team's chances of reaching the final, whatever his reasons for running on the pitch. That became even more evident when Czech referee Duan Krchnak decided to call a temporary halt while a semblance of order was restored.

NOT THIS TIME

Anderlecht goalkeeper Jaques Munaron dives bravely to deny Gary Shaw and Peter Withe

The Belgians would later claim that the hold-up had a psychological effect on them, but it was not exactly a picnic for the visitors, either. Right-back Kenny Swain, in particular, knew just how serious the situation had become. "The trouble was behind our goal, on my side of the pitch," he says. "I kept seeing the police running up and down the touchline with dogs. It got a bit hairy at times and there were obviously fears the game might have to be abandoned. If it had been re-played, I'm sure it would have enhanced Anderlecht's chances rather than ours. All of our players were on top of their game that night and it would have been difficult to do it all over again."

'I was petrified we would be kicked out of the competition.'

In the dug-out, too, the gravity of what was occurring was brought home to Villa's substitutes, whose attention was constantly distracted by riot police racing towards the trouble spots. It was, indeed, a harrowing experience in what had otherwise been a highly-enjoyable trip. Andy Blair, one of the five subs, had taken it upon himself the previous day to stroll from the club's centrally-located Hilton Hotel and admire some of the fine architecture which makes Brussels such an appealing city. The culture now unfolding in front of him was of a vastly different nature.

"The trouble was mind-blowing," he says. "I couldn't quite believe what I was seeing. It was the first time I had witnessed really bad crowd problems. I wasn't particularly concerned for my own safety, but even as it was happening I was aware there might be repercussions. I was petrified we would be kicked out of the competition."

How sad it is that so much attention was focused on the unsavoury events of a disturbing night, for Villa's performance deserved a better fate than to be overshadowed by crowd violence. Anderlecht had been the semi-final opposition they most wanted to face, but their 1-0 aggregate success was still an outstanding achievement. When the draw had been made a few weeks earlier, a collective sigh of relief had emitted over Villa Park. The presence in the last four of Bulgarians CSKA Sofia - quarter-final conquerors of Liverpool - had thrown up the possibility of yet another depressing excursion behind the Iron Curtain, while no-one relished the prospect of having to face West German giants Bayern Munich over two games.

Manager Tony Barton reflected the mood to perfection with his reaction to the semi-final pairings. "I'm happy with the draw because we shall have no travel problems or have to take our own food," he said. "I'm also pleased we avoided Bayern Munich, who are the strongest team on paper. But we would love to take them on in the final."

By the time of the first leg against Anderlecht, Barton and his right-hand man Roy MacLaren had shed their "caretaker" tags and had been officially installed as manager and assistant manager. Their trial period since Ron Saunders' resignation had brought just two defeats, with Villa moving up the First Division table as well as making progress in Europe, and chairman Ron Bendall had rewarded them accordingly.

While they had avoided both Bayern and an Iron Curtain return, however, the management team were under no illusions about the task facing them in the semi-finals. Anderlecht - or Royal Sporting Anderlechtois, to give them their full title - presented a daunting hurdle, to say the least.
Belgian champions 17 times and Cup-winners on five occasions, they had finished the previous season 11 points clear of their nearest rivals and were a team packed with internationals.

TROUBLE SPOT

The crowd disturbances which overshadowed the second leg of the semi-final and left Villa
wondering if the game would have to be re-staged

They had also won the European Cup Winners Cup twice, beating West Ham in the 1976 final and FK Austria two years later, as well as being beaten finalists in between times. Yet they were as much strangers to the Champions Cup semi-finals as Villa, never having reached this stage despite having played in the competition 11 times since its inception in 1955.

A strong feeling was growing in the EEC capital, however, that 1982 might just be Anderlecht's year, despite widespread antagonism towards coach Tomislav Ivic, whose largely negative tactics offered a stark contrast to the cavalier approach which had accompanied much of the club's earlier domestic and European success. Anyone leafing through the Villa News and Record before the first leg was certainly left in no doubt about what was in store from opponents controlled by the 49-year-old Yugoslav, who was described in the official programme as a non-smoking teetotaller who "expects rigid discipline from his players, both on and off the pitch."

"Ivic's Game" had already gained notoriety in Belgium, based as it was on a well-organised offside trap combined with mass attacking or, rather more frequently, mass defending. "It's the way kids play in school" was the description afforded Ivic's tactics by one Belgian journalist, who added ominously: "Except that discipline is unbendingly applied."

Not surprisingly, a solid defence marshalled by the coach's fellow countryman Luca Perozovic provided the foundation for Anderlecht's game plan, although it has to be said the ploy had proved far from negative in earlier rounds. Polish club Widzew Lodz, for instance, had been swept aside 6-2 on aggregate, while Italian giants Juventus and resolute Yugoslav outfit Red Star Belgrade had both been humbled 4-2 over two legs. Fourteen goals in six games hardly indicated extreme caution, and in Belgian international Willy Geurts, the team from Brussels boasted the competition's five-goal leading scorer. The skill and vision of Spanish-born Juan Lozano had also been noted by Barton and MacLaren during a spying mission across the Channel, while an abundance of other internationals meant Villa were once again confronted by formidable opponents.

Anderlecht were unlikely to be overly-concerned about coping with a vociferous Villa Park crowd, either. In the second leg of the quarter-finals they had beaten Red Star 2-1 in front of nearly 90,000 partisan Yugoslavs in Belgrade.

'If ever there was a way to kill football in 10 years...
...Ivic has found it.'

There might well have been a similar result in Birmingham, but for a fine early save by Jimmy Rimmer, who reacted smartly to push away Frank Vercauteren's goalbound shot following a swift and menacing counter attack which had opened up Villa's defence. As it transpired, however, that proved to be the visitors' single inclination to display genuine attacking adventure. They had made their intentions clear from the kick-off, employing spoiling tactics which resulted in them conceding half-a-dozen free-kicks in the opening seven minutes, and they were clearly in no mood to commit themselves unnecessarily.

The outcome, not unexpectedly, was a dour, sterile contest which prompted a scathing attack on Anderlecht's boss by Leon Hickman in the following day's *Birmingham Evening Mail*. "If ever there was a way to kill football in 10 years," Hickman wrote, "Ivic has found it. Clearly a negative thinker, he has found players of undoubted skill and turned them into a collective farm where everyone does exactly as he is told and free expression is allowed only if it is ordered. Football Communism, perhaps."

CLIMBING HIGH

Allan Evans puts the Anderlecht defence under pressure, with Peter Withe (right) waiting to pounce

Villa, having sampled enough of the real thing during their trips to Eastern Europe, had no wish to have its football equivalent thrust upon them in their own back yard, so it is no great surprise that the players have only sparse recollections of a match which was instantly forgettable. While the Belgians' spoiling tactics stifled the game's aesthetic value, however, the 28th minute goal which clinched a crucial 1-0 home victory was a classic.

Gary Williams, Gordon Cowans and Gary Shaw were all involved in a flowing move before Cowans delivered one of the most incisive passes of an illustrious career, carving open the visitors' defence with a piercing through ball which picked out Tony Morley's darting run down the left channel. The winger barely halted his stride as he controlled the ball with his right foot, advanced into the penalty area and stroked an exquisite angled left-footer beyond goalkeeper Jacky Munaron and in off the far post.

His solo effort in Berlin had been more exhilarating, but in terms of fluency and technique, Morley's fourth goal of the European campaign was a perfect blueprint for any team attempting to break down a blanket defence. It also made amends for his howler earlier in the match, and pacified a critic in the crowd. "I had a great chance in the first 10 minutes, a one-on-one with the goalkeeper," he remembers. "But I miscued my shot and it hit the corner flag! Not only was it embarrassing, it occurred to me that we weren't going to get many chances in a European semi-final against such quality opposition. As I walked back up the touchline, a supporter had a real go at me, so when I scored, I ran over and made sure I gave the guy a bit of verbal! He didn't seem too bothered, though. I think he was just delighted we were in the lead."

Manager Barton later revealed he was confident Morley's goal would be enough to secure a final place, although the Villa boss had been far from impressed with the opposition's negative approach, describing their well-regimented offside trap as "blatant" and their continual time-wasting as "unbelievable".

Despite Barton's dismay at Anderlecht's negative tactics, though, there was a rapidly-growing belief in Birmingham that Villa were destined for a final date in Rotterdam on May 26. Dennis Mortimer had suggested as much before the first leg, arguing that even a stalemate on home soil would not diminish the team's chances of going through.

"I think we have proved this season that we can play just as well away from home in this competition," he commented in a programme article. "We beat Valur in Iceland, scored twice against Dynamo Berlin in East Germany and held Dynamo Kiev to a goalless draw in Simferopol. The most important thing is that we don't go to Anderlecht trailing. Even if we are held to a draw, I shall fancy our chances of reaching the final."

The skipper's bold words were backed up by a sequence of results which saw Villa keep a clean sheet in four consecutive matches prior to the return leg. If they could extend the sequence to five in Brussels, a place in the final was assured.

Both before and after the unfortunate six-minute "time-out" at the packed Emil Verse stadium, Mortimer and his pals went about their business in a thoroughly professional manner. Ivic's Game may have been all about discipline but Villa proved in the second leg that they, too, were capable of that particular quality as they nullified the threat of Lozano and his midfield partner Ludo Coeck. With the luxury of more space than they had been afforded at home, in fact, the

MORLEY MARVEL

Tony Morley's sublime left-foot shot is on its way into the net for the goal which took Villa to the final

visitors' by-passed Anderlecht's infamous offside trap on numerous occasions and should really have extended their aggregate advantage.

Shaw was left cursing Munaron's agility when he brilliantly brought down Kenny Swain's chest-high cross with his left foot before unleashing a stinging right-foot drive which the goalkeeper tipped away for a corner. And Peter Withe was even more unfortunate. The burly striker was convinced he had put the issue beyond question when he fired an unstoppable second half shot past Munaron from just outside the penalty area, only for his glee to turn to a growl aimed at the linesman whose flag was raised for offside.

"I thought it was a great goal," Withe says. "Gordon Cowans had knocked the ball forward and Gary Shaw flicked it on. I lashed it in, giving the 'keeper no chance. When I realised the flag was up, I went mad at the linesman because I was convinced I was onside."

The controversial borderline decision meant Villa had to sweat out the closing stages with only the protection of their first leg lead, but in truth it was no great hardship. As Des Bremner points out: "They weren't able to handle our style of play. We were very quick and always closed opponents down, not allowing them to play the way they wanted. Anderlecht weren't used to that and I didn't think they were a big threat, even though we were obviously under a lot of pressure."

Indeed, Gary Williams was frequently able to make overlapping runs down the left flank, although one of his team-mates questioned the wisdom of such adventure as the tie went into its closing stages. "We had to do a lot of defending in the last 20 minutes," Williams admits.

"Even so, I was still able to get forward a fair bit, but towards the end Tony Morley yelled at me to stay back and keep things tight in defence."

At the final whistle, Barton and MacLaren bounded on to the pitch to congratulate players who were drained both physically and mentally by the night's drama, and everyone's elation was only too evident.

Allan Evans: "I was more excited that night than when we won the final. When people ask about my best memory of the competition, I always say Anderlecht because it was such an achievement to have reached the European Cup final. It gave me goosebumps."

Dennis Mortimer: "It suddenly hit me that we were in the final. I wasn't even thinking we might win it. Right at that moment, it didn't matter. I was just happy we had proved the London press wrong. They felt Ipswich Town should have won the title the year before, but we had now proved we were worthy champions."

Gordon Cowans: "The feeling at the final whistle was unbelievable, almost as good as winning the final. It was such an incredible achievement to get there. I can't begin to describe the emotion in the dressing room afterwards."

Des Bremner: "There's nothing worse in football than losing a semi-final, and having come this far we were determined it wouldn't happen to us. We just played our normal game and it was brilliant to think it had got us to the final."

Kenny Swain: We felt we had climbed our Everest when we won the semi-final. Now everyone was wondering if we could repeat it."

Tony Morley: "When the final whistle blew, I kicked the ball into the crowd and went over to our supporters to celebrate. To see the looks on Tony Barton's and Roy MacLaren's faces was wonderful."

FLYING THE FLAG
A jubilant Tony Morley salutes Villa's supporters after the goalless draw which ensured a place
in the European Cup final

Wonderful it unquestionably was, but Villa's delight would be replaced by worried frowns, not to mention a few sleepless nights, before they could contemplate making plans for Rotterdam.

It had taken them three hours of football to beat their opponents fair and square on the pitch, but Barton and his men were then forced to suffer an agonising wait of eight days before their hard-fought victory received official confirmation from European football's governing body. For just over a week after they had stoically forced a goalless draw in Brussels, Villa were left wondering whether their endeavours would be rightly rewarded by a place in the final or if they would have to go through the second leg scenario all over again.

Hundreds of fans had gone on the rampage during the crowd troubles, and with hooliganism rife in English football, there were genuine fears that UEFA would uphold Anderlecht's plea for either Villa to be expelled or the game to be re-staged. The Belgians based their claim on the six-minute hold-up which followed the one-man pitch invasion, their secretary Michael Verschueren arguing that the delay had disturbed his team's concentration. "We have nothing against Aston Villa and most of their supporters," Verschueren said. "But this kind of behaviour must be stopped."

As the tragic events in another corner of Brussels three years later would conclusively prove, such behaviour was far from being curbed. On reflection, in fact, what happened at the Emil Verse stadium was tame by comparison with the 1985 Heysel Disaster, in which 39 Juventus supporters were crushed to death while trying to escape attacks from rival fans before the final against Liverpool.

Heysel was the final straw for UEFA, who immediately banned all English clubs from competing in European competition, an exile which was to last for five years. Such a drastic measure was never a consideration after the 1982 semi-final, but Villa were understandably concerned that their opponents' protests might jeopardise their rightful place in the final. With that worry very much on their minds, they sent a deputation to the Ministry of Sport to meet sports minister Neil Macfarlane and formulate a response which heavily criticised Anderlecht's handling of the match.

The Villa party, which included FA chairman Bert Millichip, secretary Ted Croker and former Minister for Sport Denis Howell, claimed the Belgians had ignored UEFA guidelines for crowd control, sent supporters to wrong areas of the ground and failed to enforce effective segregation. Macfarlane was certainly happy with their arguments, commenting afterwards: "I am satisfied that Aston Villa followed to the letter all the UEFA ground rules on the sale of tickets and stewardship."

Eight days after the match, on Thursday April 29, Howell accompanied secretary Steve Stride to Zurich to present the club's case and await UEFA's decision, knowing that Anderlecht would claim they had been about to score when the off-duty soldier ran on to the pitch. It was a nerve-wracking experience, as Stride vividly recalls.

"I must admit I feared the worst, because I certainly couldn't recall the state of play when the match was stopped," he says. "From the moment we entered the room for that hearing in Zurich, I felt we were up against it. English clubs always seemed to be more heavily punished than other European clubs for the misbehaviour of supporters and I had the distinct impression the knives were out for us.

"Then Denis, bless him, came up with the question which ensured the game would not have to be re-staged. Anderlecht had claimed they were denied a goal by the fan running on the pitch, but Denis was a former first class referee and knew exactly what our approach should be. He simply asked where the game had been re-started and the answer was that it had resumed just inside our half. The Belgians could hardly argue they were about to break through our defence from there."

Villa were fined 50,000 Swiss francs and ordered to play their next European home game behind closed doors, but while the punishment hit them in the pocket, their financial losses represented a gentle rap across the knuckles by comparison with what they stood to lose. Their place in the final was assured. It was time to start preparing for the biggest match in the club's history.

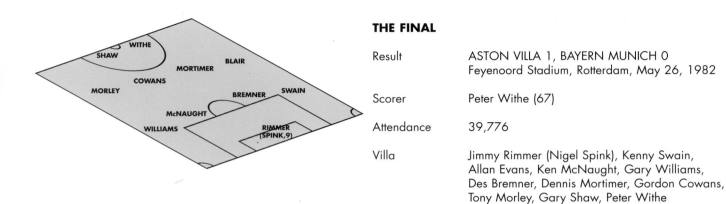

THE FINAL

Result	**ASTON VILLA 1, BAYERN MUNICH 0** Feyenoord Stadium, Rotterdam, May 26, 1982
Scorer	Peter Withe (67)
Attendance	39,776
Villa	Jimmy Rimmer (Nigel Spink), Kenny Swain, Allan Evans, Ken McNaught, Gary Williams, Des Bremner, Dennis Mortimer, Gordon Cowans, Tony Morley, Gary Shaw, Peter Withe Subs (not used): Andy Blair, Colin Gibson, Pat Heard, David Geddis
Bayern	Manfred Muller, Wolfgang Dremmler, Udo Horsmann, Hans Weiner, Klaus Augenthaler, Wolfgang Kraus (Kurt Niedermayer), Bernhard Durnberger, Paul Breitner, Deiter Hoeness, Reinhold Mathy (Gunther Guttler), Karl-Hienz Rummenigge
Referee	Georges Konrath (France)

The Magnificent Mis-hit

Goal of the Season? No chance. Goal of the Month? Not a hope. Let's be honest, it was only Goal of the Game because there were no other contenders. Peter Withe couldn't have cared less. With arguably the most awkward contact of his career, he had claimed the most significant goal in Aston Villa's history, the one which made them kings of Europe. Needless to say, the Magnificent Mis-hit is etched indelibly on his mind.

"I can remember it as if it happened yesterday," he insists. "Tony Morley turned a defender one way and then the other. Klaus Augenthaler was marking me but he sensed the danger and moved across to cover, which left me on my own as I reached the six-yard box.

"Tony drove the ball hard across the goalmouth but it seemed to happen in slow motion and I said to myself: 'Concentrate!' The ball hit a divot as it reached me and it half hit my shin and half hit my ankle before flying against the post and in. I'm convinced that if I'd struck it properly, the 'keeper would have saved it, but he didn't expect that. I was too close to the goal to run to our supporters, so I ran into the net to celebrate. Gary Shaw was the first to reach me and then Gordon Cowans jumped on my neck and dragged me to the ground. I must have resisted a bit because he kept saying: "Get down, you bastard!'"

Cowans' forceful utterance was very much a term of endearment, echoed by team-mates who were ecstatic about taking the lead against mighty Bayern Munich in the European Cup final. All the same, Withe's goal has been the butt of some affectionate mickey-taking down the years. Cowans, a keen golfer, describes the crucial strike as "a shank", adding: "Withey did his best to miss it, but somehow it went in!"

Given Withe's penchant for scorching left-foot shots, it came as quite a surprise that the most important goal of his impressive collection should be struck with his right leg, albeit in an unconventional manner. Des Bremner jokes: "Withey obviously decided not to hit it with his left peg and make too good a goal of it. He didn't score too many with his right, and watching that one, you could see why! But it doesn't matter how they go in, and it was marvellous that Peter scored at the end where our supporters were massed."

If the finish was an haphazard, almost apologetic affair, maybe the sheer cheek of it reflects Villa's approach to the biggest game of their lives. They had every right to be on tenterhooks about the prospect of facing West German aristocrats in European club football's showpiece, but if there was any nervous tension lurking just beneath the surface, it never became evident. It is tempting to suggest the players deliberately suppressed their anxiety, but the truth is that they were genuinely relaxed about the whole thing.

The one exception, perhaps, was Kenny Swain, who admits that despite the buoyant mood among his team-mates, he was a little on edge about playing in the European Cup final. "Before the final I thought: 'I'm 30 and this chance will probably never come along again.' I wanted to make sure I was both physically and mentally prepared so I went to the training ground before we flew out to Rotterdam and had a run, just to shed a couple of pounds. The league season had finished only a few days earlier but I wanted to make sure I was in peak condition before we started training for the final. I also went out for a run by myself the night before the game, just to make absolutely sure. My philosophy was that if I failed, I didn't want to look back with any regrets over the way I had prepared."

Once Swain arrived at the Feyenoord Stadium on the night of the match, his nerves evaporated into the steeply-rising arena known in Rotterdam as De Kuip - "the tub" - as he savoured the build-up with his pals. There was almost a carefree air about the Villa party as they took in the surroundings and waved to wives and girlfriends before one or two of them produced cameras and started taking photographs of each other on the pitch. Those moments of simply soaking up the atmosphere and relishing the big occasion have remained fresh in so many minds, long after specific details of the match itself have faded from memory. Just in case the feeling of well-being needs spelling out, this sample of pre-match recollections should do the trick:

Des Bremner: "You wouldn't have thought it was a European Cup final. A few of the lads had cameras with them and before the game we were all taking photos of each other. We were just laughing and joking. The Germans had been out on the pitch an hour for a warm-up an hour before the kick-off and as we walked past their dressing room it all seemed very serious in there. You could see the tension in their faces, while our lads were just cracking jokes. For us, it was something just to be there."

Pat Heard: "I wanted some souvenirs, so I took my camera to Rotterdam and that was picked up by Brian Clough, who was commentating on the game for ITV with Brian Moore. During his commentary, Clough said: 'I can't believe this team have come to a European Cup final. We've had players on the pitch, taking photographs of each other!' I was only on the bench but there didn't seem to be any fear among the lads who were playing."

Allan Evans: "Looking around the faces of our players, you could tell they couldn't believe we were there. But there was no real tension about us, no fear. We wanted to

ASTON VILLA
FOOTBALL CLUB PLC
Registered Office:
Villa Park, Birmingham B6 6HE
Telephone: 021-327 6604

AstonVilla

FROM:

ITINERARY FOR STAFF PLANE
* * * * * * * * * *
EUROPEAN CUP FINAL

26 May 1982

BAYERN MUNICH v ASTON VILLA

WEDNESDAY, 26 May - 11.00hrs

11.30hrs

13.30hrs

15.35hrs
(local time)

Report Villa Park for coaches to airport (anyone wishing to travel direct to Birmingham Airport please notify Comme Department).

Check-in British Midlands desk at Birmingham Airpor

Depart Birmingham Airpo

Arrive Amsterdam

Coaches will transfer your hotel accommoda Amsterdam where you have enough time to and deposit your ba

Coaches will then the Stadium in Ro

Immediately following the end of the match you will transfer again to the private coaches to report to your hotel.

Depart from Ho at Amsterdam 12.00 noon.

Depart Ams

THURSDAY, 27 May - 11.30hrs

13.35hrs
(local time)

13.40hrs

Arrive B
Coaches
for tho
return

DON'T FORGET YOUR PASSPOR

Vice-Chairman
Don Bendall

Directors
Harry Kartz, Trevor Gill

Registered No. 46572 England

Manager
Tony Barton

66

THAT'S MINE

A confident Nigel Spink leaps to collect a Bayern cross, guarded by Des Bremner (left) and Ken McNaught

win the game, but it was a big thing just to be in the final. Tony Barton helped to keep us relaxed because he seemed totally laid back about it all."

Andy Blair: "We were quite calm about the whole thing. We just took it in our stride. We arrived at the stadium in smart new blazers and I couldn't help thinking the Bayern players looked like tramps. It seemed they weren't treating the occasion with the respect it deserved. Yet we were probably more relaxed than they were, even though we were suited up. I always carried a camera with me and took lots of photos. The atmosphere was brilliant."

'The Germans were warming up and I wasn't even in the ground.'

Tony Morley: "There were no nerves. We knew we were playing the *creme de la creme* of European football and really had nothing to lose, so we were quite relaxed. We went shopping the day before the game and even had a few beers - nothing too heavy, of course - and there was no pressure on us. I didn't even get changed until 20 minutes before kick-off. Some lads I knew wanted tickets for the game, so I met them outside the stadium. The Germans were warming up, and I wasn't even in the ground! The guys I had got the tickets for were a bit concerned about that, and asked if I was playing but I told them it would only take me 10 minutes to get changed. I never liked being ready a long time before a game."

Gary Williams: "Our wives came out to Rotterdam on the day of the game and I managed to see Liz. When she asked how I was feeling and I said "fine", she couldn't believe how calm I was. It was possibly the same for the other younger players. The likes of Gary Shaw and myself had only been in the side for three years, yet in our second season we had won the League and now we were in the European Cup final. To us, it seemed that this was how things were all the time."

By the latter stages of the competition, Villa's starting line-up virtually picked itself and the only real poser for Barton before the final was to select his five substitutes. His choice was slightly controversial, Colin Gibson being given one of the five shirts despite not having played any senior football for almost four months, while two more obvious contenders, Brendan Ormsby and Mark Jones, travelled to Rotterdam but had to watch from the stand.

The decision was possibly based on sentiment, Gibson having been a regular in the side before suffering a pelvic strain in a 4-1 defeat by Manchester United at Old Trafford in February on the 25th anniversary of the Munich Air Disaster. Whatever the reason for his inclusion, Gibson was more than grateful, even if it left him with mixed emotions.

"I'd played 35 games non-stop until I was injured but on the Sunday morning after the United match, I couldn't even get out of bed," he recalls. "After that, I obviously wasn't going to be fit for the Dynamo Kiev and Anderlecht ties. It was annoying, because I had been first choice all season, but Gary Williams did tremendously well when he took over.

"I eventually got myself fit about two weeks before the end of the season but I didn't get back in the first team and I thought I was going to miss out in the final. I had a feeling Mark Jones would be on the bench, but Tony gave me the nod. That was a relief, but when it came to the night of the match I felt gutted because I knew if I hadn't been injured I would have been wearing the No 3 shirt. That was a real disappointment but it was even worse for Mark because he didn't even get a medal.

GOOD EVANS

Allan Evans heads clear from a left wing cross as Ken McNaught keeps a close watch on Dieter Hoeness

"My emotions that night were topsy-turvy, to say the least. The atmosphere around the stadium was magical and our fans seemed to outnumber Bayern's by a long way. But I didn't enjoy the moment as much as I should have done because of that nagging feeling I should really have been playing. I didn't really get involved in the thing, which was a bit of immaturity on my part and something I've always regretted."

There were mixed feelings, too, for Ormsby who, like Gibson, had played in the opening rounds but now had a substitute's shirt as his only ambition. In the event, he didn't even manage that, although his initial anger eventually gave way to an appreciation of what the occasion meant.

"Mark Jones and myself were both in the travelling party but we had to sit in the stand with all the wives and girlfriends," he says. "To be honest, I was really pissed off because I felt I was worth a place, but when I went out on the pitch before the match and saw all the Villa fans, it lifted my mood. It suddenly dawned on me that this wasn't about Brendan Ormsby but about Aston Villa. Not being in the 16 meant Mark and I didn't get a medal. The club said they would get us a memento of the occasion but I didn't want that because I didn't feel I'd earned it."

Arriving in the Dutch seaport two days before the match, Villa had gone through their preparations for the final at the training ground of a local amateur team, their work-outs attracting around 200 spectators, who made it clear they would be backing Barton's Boys to beat "the Germans". Once again, however, it was going to be anything but easy. Bayern, three times winners of the trophy during the 1970s, overflowed with talented individuals, including classy sweeper Klaus Augenthaler, lethal marksman Dieter Hoeness, inspirational skipper Paul Breitner and European player-of-the-year Karl-Hienz Rummenigge. They had sounded an ominous warning, too, with a scintillating semi-final display against CSKA Sofia, recovering from a 4-3 first leg deficit to trounce the Bulgarians 7-4 on aggregate.

'Go on Spinksy, you'll be all right. Don't let one in!'

Yet there was a quiet belief in the Villa camp that their name was on the cup, and Dennis Mortimer had particularly good reason for wanting to get his hands on it. "In the week leading up to the final, I started thinking about how Liverpool and Nottingham Forest and won the previous five finals between them," he says. "It occurred to me: 'Why not us?' I'd seen Phil Thompson lift the trophy for Liverpool, and he was in the year below me at school - Brookfield Secondary in Kirkby. I started to imagine what it would be like for that school to have two former pupils lifting the European Cup."

During the flight to Holland, the crew of the KLM DC-8 plane had been in equally upbeat mood, telling Villa's players and officials: "You *will* win the cup." Such votes of confidence are not uncommon from airline crews taking English teams to matches overseas, but Mortimer and his men vowed during that flight to transform the bold prediction into reality.

Just nine minutes into the final, Villa's self-belief was tested to the limit. No-one had paid a great deal of attention the previous day when Jimmy Rimmer had ricked his neck in training, and even when he was given two pain-killing injections before kick-off, it barely raised a comment. But with the match still settling down, Gary Williams suddenly became aware that all was not well with the experienced goalkeeper. "I was the first to realise something was wrong," the full-back recalls. "Jimmy shouted at me 'I need to come off' and I couldn't believe what I was hearing. It came as quite a shock."

YOU PUT BOTH ARMS IN
Nigel Spink engages in a Rotterdam version of the hokey-cokey with a Bayern player

It was, indeed, a surprise to the whole team that such an important member of the side should have to leave the field with the action barely under way. Even Barton and his assistant MacLaren were taken aback, despite having known about Rimmer's injury. As the manager later revealed: "We did not take a calculated gamble in playing him because a decision of fitness can only be left to the player. He's the one who really knows. Jimmy said he was okay and I was perfectly satisfied because he had gone through an intensive work-out that morning without any sign of discomfort."

'The last thing I wanted was to go on and foul things up.'

The secret had certainly been well-kept but now it was out in the open, the only option was to send on 23-year-old Nigel Spink, whose football during the 1981-82 campaign had amounted to 36 Central League matches for Villa's reserves. But if the dramatic switch created a few flutters in the English camp, Spink's fellow substitutes did their best to put him at ease.

"When Jimmy waved across to the bench, we were all thinking: 'What on earth is he doing?'" says Andy Blair. "It was a complete surprise but we said to Spinksy: 'You're on here, mate.' Although it was a blow that Jimmy had to come off, maybe it was a catalyst for the rest of the team, who obviously felt they had to protect a young goalkeeper who had hardly played at first team level."

Pat Heard recalls: "I was Nigel's room-mate. Even when he had to go on he didn't seem too worried. We just joked with him and said: 'Go on, Spinksy, you'll be all right. Don't let one in!' Somehow I just knew he would be okay. I'd played in the reserves with him for a long time and I knew exactly what he could do."

The boy from Chelmsford did everything that was asked of him, and more. When he entered the cauldron of the European Cup final, his first team experience amounted to all of 90 minutes, and that had been two-and-a-half years earlier, but his performance in Rotterdam made him an instant hero.

Barely had he taken up his position between the posts than he was required to collect a long, speculative forward punt. It was a routine save, but as Brian Clough observed in his role as ITV summariser, the Germans did Spink a huge favour at that moment, providing him with a welcome early feel of the ball from which his confidence escalated as the game progressed.

Nearly half-an-hour elapsed before Spink was more seriously tested, but the confident manner in which the stand-in 'keeper dived to his right to hold Bernhard Durnberger's low drive set a pattern which would lay the foundations for Villa's victory. Spink made numerous other saves in a one-sided second half, and even when he was wrong-footed by Augenthaler's far post header, Swain was perfectly positioned to clear off the line.

JUST TOO HIGH
Tony Morley unleashes Villa's first shot of the second half but his effort flies over the bar.
Two minutes later, he would make a rather more dramatic contribution...

"The great thing for Nigel is that he made a couple of good saves, which settled him down," says Mortimer. "If one of those had gone in, it could have been curtains for us because it would have destroyed his confidence. Instead, he grew in stature as the match went on."

Peter Withe agrees: "Even though he had played only one first team match, Nigel had a reputation as a good shot-stopper and most of his saves that night required the sort of reaction in which he specialised. Despite being a tall guy, he was very good at getting down to low shots and he had to deal with one or two of those in Rotterdam."

Despite his heroics, Spink knew little about a superb first half overhead kick from Rummenigge which flashed only inches past his left-hand post and brought gasps of admiration from all around the stadium - including some of Villa's players.

Allan Evans: "I had the job of marking Rummenigge and to play against a player like that was a big thrill for me. When he put in that free-kick, it must have been only a few centimetres wide. I thought 'That was magnificent' and I actually felt like applauding. I was playing against him, and I obviously wanted to win, but that was sheer class."

'Have I really done that? Was I really there that night?'

Kenny Swain: "Even though Bayern were favourites, I wasn't really sure how good they were, but I revised my thinking after that shot. Paul Breitner hit a cross which went over me and Allan Evans and as I looked round I saw Rummenigge leap up and send an overhead kick just past the post. It suddenly dawned on me: 'Swainy, you've underestimated this lot!' They were obviously world class players and I started to wonder if we had a chance. But Nigel was tremendous when he came on and the only time he was beaten, I headed off the line."

If Spink's heroics were a major factor in Villa's triumph, an early tactical switch also contributed significantly to quelling the German spearhead. Ken McNaught: "Bayern had big reputations, but they were like bits of cardboard, the way they stuck so rigidly to their system. Allan Evans and I used to take sides, and if the opposition only played with one striker, he would mark the guy and I would pick up the pieces. But we were very flexible. After a few minutes of the final we realised that Hoeness was outjumping Allan and Rummenigge was outstripping me. So we decided to go man-for-man with our marking, and it worked."

For all their resilience, Villa were forced to endure some anxious moments as the final drew agonisingly slowly towards its conclusion, and the strain began to show on one or two players. Tony Morley recalls Gordon Cowans leaning on a post, looking physically and mentally drained as Bayern prepared to take a corner, and it briefly looked as if a second substitution might have to be made. The fact that it didn't happen was a relief both to Gary Williams and the man who would have replaced him, Colin Gibson.

"Towards the end I had a sore knee and my socks were rolled down," says Williams. "I was probably tired from getting forward too much in the

I'M GOING THIS WAY

Tony Morley throws Hans Weiner off balance with a brilliant body swerve before crossing for
Peter Withe to score the winner

first half. I saw Colin warming up on the touchline but there was no way I was coming off. I wanted to be on that pitch when the final whistle went."

Gibson recalls: "When Gary went down, I thought for a minute I would be going on. I got pretty nervous just then because I hadn't played a first team game since February and in one way it was quite a relief when Gary got up. It would have been nice to have the chance of playing some small part in the final, but the last thing I wanted was to go on and foul things up."

Villa's fatigue was never more evident than three minutes from time when they were caught out by a long through ball from Kurt Niedermayer which was headed on by Gunther Guttler before Hoeness drilled a low shot which skidded past Spink and inside the left-hand post. All their earlier endeavours, it seemed, had been for nothing and they would have to play 30 minutes of extra-time. But no. A linesman's flag was raised to indicate that Hoeness was offside when the ball was headed forward.

Much to the Germans' dismay and Villa's delight, the effort was disallowed, but the contrast in reactions to that decision was nothing by comparison with the teams' response to the final whistle. Bayern may have been more dominant, but Villa had scored the only goal to become champions of Europe. While the Germans gathered dejectedly in the centre-circle, Barton's boys went running to their supporters to savour a triumph many of the players or fans had never even dreamed of.

'We got away with a lot that night but it didn't matter because we won the cup.'

"We got away with a lot that night but it didn't matter because we won the cup," says Allan Evans. "I swapped shirts with Rummenigge and as I went up the steps to collect my medal, I saw the German players sitting around the centre-circle, looking dejected. I couldn't understand why Rummenigge felt so bad, because he had my shirt! Seriously, though, you had to enjoy moments like that because you knew there would be other times when you would taste defeat. Right after the final whistle, Gary Newbon grabbed me for a television interview, and I didn't know what I was saying. The adrenaline was flowing and emotions were so high that I just didn't care what I said."

Tony Morley: "When the whistle went, it was an amazing feeling. As a kid, I'd watched Manchester United win the European Cup and I'd always wondered what it would be like. It suddenly occurred to me that we were now part of football history. I was last off the pitch with the cup because it dawned on me I might never do this again and I wanted to savour every last moment of it. I suddenly realised how much joy we had brought to so many people."

Des Bremner: "When the final whistle went, it was brilliant, although I don't think I quite realised just what a big thing it was to have won the European Cup. It was only with the passing of years that I realised how well we had done. Bayern were the better team, but that's by-the-by."

Victory was special for the whole of the team and, indeed, the rest of the squad, but particularly so for the man with the honour of being presented with the cup. Skipper Dennis Mortimer, though, had to be patient before he could hold aloft that prestigious piece of silverware.

"All I could think of in the last few minutes was getting my hands on that trophy," he recalls. "When the final whistle went, it was joy, joy, joy. We had proved all the critics wrong and shown our title success the previous year had been no fluke.

IN OFF THE POST
Peter Withe's magnificent mis-hit beats Bayern goalkeeper Manfred Muller to clinch Villa's
history-making victory

"I couldn't wait to get up those stairs to collect the cup, but all the lads were behind the goal, celebrating with our fans. One of the UEFA delegates came over to me and asked if I could gather all the players together and I thought: 'You must be joking!'

'All I could think of in the last few minutes was getting my hands on the trophy.'

"Thankfully, the lads all came back, realising there was a trophy and a medal to collect and once I was holding the cup, I didn't want to let it go. I kept it in my hands as long as possible to make sure there were lots of photographs of me ! To have won such a prestigious tournament was wonderful, and to be holding the cup was a dream within a dream. Every time I watch the final on TV, I always find it a special moment when the trophy is presented. I think: 'Yes, I've been there, done that.' It still gives me a magical feeling."

Similar emotions have lingered with midfielder Pat Heard. He was one of the players who didn't kick a ball throughout the competition, but his inclusion among the substitutes in Rotterdam meant he collected a treasured winners' medal. There are occasions, he admits, when he still finds it hard to contemplate that he was part of such a momentous achievement.

"Sometimes, I find it hard to believe what happened," he says. "When I watch the final on television, I keep thinking: 'Have I really done that? Was I really there that night?' When you think that clubs spend millions of pounds trying to win the European Cup, I find it difficult to comprehend that I have a winners' medal. Even though I didn't play, it was a terrific feeling just to be there and be part of it."

If Villa could barely believe what they had achieved, neutral observers in this country were also trying to figure out how the English champions had triumphed against the odds. Bayern had been quoted as 5-4 ON favourites to lift the trophy and had unquestionably been the better team, but Ron Atkinson came up with the reason the bookies got it wrong.

Atkinson, who would manage Villa a decade later, was then in charge of Manchester United and was working that night in London as a summariser alongside ITV presenter Dickie Davies. He made the point that Bayern, and skipper Paul Breitner in particular, had totally misjudged their opponents' approach to the game.

"Breitner was saying he thought Villa didn't play in a typical English side," Atkinson said in his post-match appraisal. "But he has been beaten tonight by a side who have displayed one of the greatest assets in the British game, and that's guts. As a technical exercise, you have to say Villa's win was against the run of play. In the second half in particular, the Germans were streets ahead in terms of technique. But it terms of guts and character, Villa have done it all tonight."

FC BAYERN-ASTON VILLA 0-1

THE FINAL COUNTDOWN
Nigel Spink makes another save with the scoreboard showing the final score as the seconds tick away

WE'VE DONE IT
Nigel Spink and Tony Morley celebrate as they wait to collect the prize

THANKS, FANS
Manager Tony Barton salutes Villa's supporters at the final whistle, while Peter Withe
gets ready to party

YESSSS!!
Gary Williams and Gordon Cowans show their delight to the
travelling Villa fans

STAIRWAY TO HEAVE
Dennis Mortimer, still in his wh
shirt, proudly holds aloft t
European Cup. Some of
colleagues have alrea
swapped shirts w
Bayern playe

Gary Shaw finds a resting place for the trophy - on top of Tony Morley's head

PETER'S PRIDE
His face a picture of delight, goalscorer Peter Withe clutches the coveted European Cup after
swapping shirts with an opponent

A Tale Of Two Keepers

Whenever people recall the 1982 European Cup final, one incident immediately springs to mind. Peter Withe's goal may have clinched victory, but the biggest talking point in Rotterdam was undoubtedly the dramatic replacement of Jimmy Rimmer by substitute Nigel Spink after only nine minutes. This is how the two goalkeepers remember the big night

JIMMY RIMMER

I hardly touched the ball before coming off, but I knew after only two or three minutes that I wasn't going to be able to play the whole of the final.

Rummenigge hit a shot from long range and although it went well wide, I realised that if he'd been on target, I wouldn't have got there. I couldn't lift my arm properly, and I knew that if someone hit a low shot, I wouldn't be able to get down in time.

The next few minutes were mental agony as I decided what to do. Luckily, we kept Bayern pretty quiet in the opening stages and apart from throwing the ball out to Gary Williams a couple of times, I wasn't troubled. But I realised it was useless tryng to continue, and I shouted to Gary to let the manager know.

That was the hardest thing I ever had to do as a footballer and I can't even begin to explain how devastated I was. My wife Chris was in the stands and the rest of my family were watching at home on television. I'd played in every other game, conceding only two goals, and this should have been the crowning point of my career, but it was all over after only nine minutes.

I felt so dejected that I couldn't even watch the rest of the first half. Doc Targett took me into the dressing room and I just sat there with tears streaming down my face. It was only when the other lads came in and half-time and started talking about how the game was going that I snapped out of my depression.

Thankfully I was back on the touchline - with a collar on my neck - in time to see Peter's winning goal and at least I got a medal. But it took me quite a while to get over the disappointment of not having played the full 90 minutes of what should have been the biggest game of my life.

I'd actually been aware since the previous Friday that there might be a problem. Bob Latchford had backed into me as we challenged for a cross to the near post during our final league match against Swansea, and I'd fallen awkwardly on my neck.

The injury was kept a secret and I know Tony Barton was anxious for me to play in the final because Nigel had next to no first team experience. I had some treatment over the weekend and I did very little training when we got to Rotterdam, but I woke up at in the early hours on the day of the final and I just couldn't move my neck.

Maybe I should have realised then that I wasn't going to make it, but I was determined not to let anyone down. After a couple of pain-killing injections, I felt okay and when we went out of the pitch before the match I was confident I could get through it.

But that early shot from Rummenigge made me realise I was kidding myself. All these years later, I still get pain in my neck from time to time. But it doesn't hurt half as much as having to come off after nine minutes of the European Cup final.

JIMMY'S AGONY
Tony Barton and Roy MacLaren try to console Jimmy Rimmer as he leaves the field

NIGEL SPINK

When I went on, it came totally out of the blue. I didn't have a clue that Jimmy had a problem. He was one of those goalkeepers who always had a strapping on some part of his body, so people never questioned if he was fit. I didn't think for one minute that he wouldn't play the whole of the final, so I was very relaxed in the build-up.

I'd been out on the pitch an hour before kick-off to warm-up and I decided to make the most of that. I wanted to get as much of the atmosphere as possible. I wanted to get a good sweat on, and enjoy it as much as I could because I didn't think for a minute I would be involved. That warm-up probably did me good when I had to go on.

It came as a shock to everyone when Jimmy came off. He decided he had a problem and didn't want to let the team down, so he made the brave decision to call it a day. It was a big decision having to come off in a European Cup final, particularly after all the work he had done and the great displays he had given in previous rounds. His form was important in getting us there in the first place. It certainly wouldn't have happened without him.

I was just told, 'Get ready, you're on'. It was starting to cool down but it was still very humid. There was no time for nerves and I'm sure that had a lot to do with what happened. I got a couple of good early touches and from that point I was able to play my normal game.

Apart from one match at Forest, I'd only played reserve football until that moment and it was quite a departure from the almost deserted stadiums I was used to. I'd been in the reserves the best part of three years and I felt I had served an apprenticeship.

When I went on, I was lucky enough to make important saves at important times. The first one was a confidence-booster because I got down quickly and held on to the ball. Then they broke through and had a close-range shot which I parried.

By half-time, I'd settled down and I was itching to get out there again for the second half. It was a fairy tale, incredible, unbelievable. I still watch the match on video savour every minute of it.

COME IN No.19
The final is over for Jimmy Rimmer after only nine minutes, but Nigel Spink's face reflects his sheer determination as he takes over in goal

The Cup In The Loo

"Excuse me, gentlemen, would you mind walking this way?" It wasn't exactly the long arm of the law which beckoned, but Peter Withe and Ken McNaught knew their number was up. Only in the eyes of Bayern Munich had they committed any sort of crime, having robbed the lords of Bavaria what they regarded as their rightful claim to the European throne. UEFA delegates attending the final made no such allegation against Villa's match-winner and his defensive colleague, but were nevertheless anxious to establish that victory had been achieved without any outside influences.

UEFA's regulations stipulated that two players from each team should undergo post-match tests to ensure no banned substances had been used, and the random selection threw up numbers nine and five. Within minutes of the teams leaving the field at the Feyenoord Stadium, the Villa duo, together with their Bayern counterparts Dieter Hoeness and Klaus Augenthaler, were duly whisked away to provide the required urine samples.

Understandably, Withe and McNaught would have preferred to continue with the dressing room frolics which inevitably followed such a famous victory, but their celebrations would have to wait - much longer, in fact, than either of them could possibly have anticipated.

"After the match, myself and Ken were told we had to go for random drugs tests," says Withe. "We were taken to a two-berth caravan under the stand and they gave us phialls into which we were supposed to provide samples. Hoeness and Augenthaler were in there as well, but no-one could manage anything for a while because we had all sweat so much.

"We looked out of the caravan window and someone was walking past with a crate of beer. We asked where he was taking it and he said it was for the Villa dressing room, so we hijacked it! We drank about four beers each, but it took ages before it had the desired effect. I managed it first, so I went and sat in the bath with a glass of Champagne, but it was quite a while before Ken came back to the dressing room. Then someone came in and told us that if we didn't hurry up, the coach would be leaving without us and we would have to get a taxi to Amsterdam for the banquet. Luckily we just made it."

At least the Liverpool-born striker was quicker off the mark than his Scottish team-mate, enabling him to savour a drop of bubbly before getting changed. McNaught's escape from the drug-testing caravan took rather longer. "A guy brought in some Pepsi and lemonade to help us along," the defender recalls. "But Peter and I looked at each other and told him our season was now over, could we please have something a little more satisfying! The beer seemed to do the trick, but it still took quite a while and I took longer than Peter - which shows I had obviously done a lot more running than him! By the time I eventually got showered and changed, everyone else was on the bus."

While Withe and McNaught were doing their duty for the medical men, the rest of the team had followed up their dressing room high jinks with a welcome soak in the bath, yet once their initial euphoria had subsided, the mood was strangely subdued. Pat Heard describes the scene: "After the game, our wives and girlfriends went off to Amsterdam but we had to wait in a bar in the stadium while Ken and Peter had their tests. It was unreal. We had just won the European Cup but we just sat around, having a beer and chatting. We were just like a bunch of lads enjoying a drink after a Sunday League game."

It was a different story once the victorious squad had finally embarked on the hour-long journey to Amsterdam, where a post-match banquet had been arranged for all the club's staff and their partners at the Apollo Hotel. The coach had barely reached the outskirts of Rotterdam when the joviality returned with a vengeance.

Even Brendan Ormsby, bitterly disappointed at having had to watch from the stand, was carried along on the second wave of celebration, establishing himself as the life and soul of the party as his favourite music blasted from the coach's sound system. "I love Elvis Presley and the driver put on one of his tapes," says Ormsby. "That really got us going and I have a photo of myself, Swainy and Withey doing Elvis impersonations."

For the first few kilometres, too, the cup was passed around and proudly clutched by every member of the squad, but eventually a tricky problem arose - where to put the huge, top-heavy trophy to prevent it from falling over. Empty seats and the floor of the coach were both tried with no success, but Heard still treasures his unique photograph of the cup in an unlikely setting for the remainder of the journey.

"After everyone had enjoyed holding it, no-one wanted the responsibility of keeping it upright," he says. "Wherever we put it, it kept falling over. Then someone came up with the bright idea of putting it in the toilet! That's where it stayed until we got to Amsterdam."

It's hard to imagine that the European Cup has ever been consigned to the loo, either before Villa's Dutch coach journey or since, and the players were in such jovial mood by the time they reached the Apollo Hotel, they actually left it in its unusual resting place. Luckily, it was soon retrieved, and the biggest party in Villa's history was under way.

"When we arrived in Amsterdam and everyone got off the bus, Tony Barton suddenly asked where the trophy was," says Ken McNaught. "Tony and myself had to get back on the bus, and we eventually found the cup standing up in the loo!

"Once we were inside the hotel, myself and one of the porters filled up the cup with Champagne and took it around the room, telling people they could take the easy option of a glass of bubbly, or risk having a drink from the trophy. Everyone joined in the spirit of the occasion, but the Champagne was like a tidal wave coming at them as it gushed out of the cup and splashed everywhere. A few expensive dresses and club blazers got drenched that night!"

'I had to grab her to stop her falling out of the window.'

Getting wet was the least of Peter Withe's problems. The striker had to make a save which would have done Nigel Spink proud. "We filled the cup with 26 bottles of Champagne and everyone had a swig," Withe recalls. "My wife Kathy was sitting on a ledge near an open window and the cup was so heavy that she lost balance and slipped as she tried to have a drink. I had to grab her to stop her falling out of the window!"

Even Allan Evans, a tee-totaller who simply doesn't like the taste of alcohol, indulged in the sweet taste of glory before settling down to watch his team-mates getting more and more drunk as the long night of celebration wore on, but another member of Villa's non-drinking fraternity was thrown into a state of panic during the festivities.

"I misplaced my medal twice that night and I was worried I had lost it," says Andy Blair. "I can't even blame the drink, because I'm tee-total. Thankfully, I found it both times and I was determined

AT FULL STRETCH
Nigel Spink relaxes at Schipol airport before boarding the flight home from Amsterdam

to savour the whole thing. I was thrilled to be a part of it, even though I hadn't played. My parents were there, too. Everyone was allowed to invite a partner to the banquet, but I didn't have a girlfriend at the time so mum and dad came along. They loved every minute of it and I was delighted that they were able to share it with me."

Blair and Gary Shaw also attracted a few envious glances from the club's married fraternity when, with the dinner formally concluded, they left the hotel and headed off in the direction of Amsterdam's famous Red Light area - purely out of curiosity, of course! "I didn't want the night to end," admits Shaw. "We walked around the Red Light district and had a few drinks. It was about 5am when we got back to the hotel."

A few hours later, the celebrations resumed, but this time it was a men-only affair. "It's fair to say most of us had hangovers the following morning," says Colin Gibson. "While our wives and girlfriends were still around, we acted like gentlemen, but they had to leave the hotel a couple of hours before us because they were booked on an earlier flight. Once we had waved them off, and their coach had disappeared around the corner, someone shouted 'Come on, let's get back in the bar!' It was a bit early in the day for drinking, but we didn't need much persuading. Funnily

'When we landed I discovered he had cut a chunk of my hair!'

enough, our wives' plane was delayed, so they were still at the airport when we got there. They must have wondered what had been happening because we were all the worse for wear again!"

Gary Williams was more dishevelled than most, even though he had taken things easy the previous night - and he paid the price in the form of an unwanted haircut. "I had drunk so much Coca Cola after the game that I had actually felt sick on the coach journey to Amsterdam," he recalls. "Everyone else was having a good time but I just sat there, feeling rough. Even at the dinner, I didn't feel too well. Apart from a mouthful of Champagne from the cup, I didn't have a drink all night.

"It was only the following morning that it started to sink in what we had achieved and I began to enjoy myself. I was feeling much better by then, so I joined the other lads in the bar after our wives and girlfriends had left. But I obviously overdid it. On the flight back home I went to sleep, which was a big mistake because I was sitting in front of Peter Withe. When we landed, I discovered he had cut a chunk of my hair! It was quite long at the time, but I suddenly had a bald spot on the back of my head."

Williams was not the only one to fall victim to a practical joke during the return flight. As the plane touched down at East Midlands airport, Gordon Cowans was alarmed to discover he had mislaid his medal. "I was crawling around on the plane, looking for it," he recalls. "But there was no sign of it anywhere and I started to panic. I was close to tears by the time we got to our coach because I thought it was lost, but Tony Morley was sitting there, having a little giggle to himself. It turned out he'd had the medal all along. I didn't think it was too funny at the time, but I was relieved to get it back. It's one of my most treasured possessions and I've kept is safe ever since."

The following afternoon, Villa rounded off their celebrations with an open-top bus ride through the streets of Birmingham, followed by a Civic Reception at the Council House. Thousands of fans packed into Victoria Square to salute their heroes, while others clambered on to rooftops for a better view of the proceedings.

CAPTAIN'S LOG
Dennis Mortimer in the cockpit with Captain Nederlof before the homeward flight

It was the second time in 12 months that Villa's players had savoured such adulation, although there were two notable absentees from the squad who had celebrated the club's 1981 League Championship triumph.

Having savoured the sweet taste of victory in Rotterdam, Allan Evans had been forced to say farewell to his team-mates at the airport the following day because his season was far from over. "I had been picked for Scotland's World Cup squad and we had a warm-up match against England at Hampden Park on the Saturday," he recalls. "Instead of flying back with the Villa lads. I flew direct to Glasgow for the match. After everything we had been through together, I would have loved to be there for the open top bus ride and the chance to see all the fans gathered. It had been a great occasion when we had a Civic Reception after winning the league and I was really disappointed at missing out on the second one."

While Evans was north of the border as Villa paraded their prestigious piece of silverware, Eamonn Deacy was on the other side of the Atlantic. The genial Irishman had also enjoyed the previous year's celebrations as one of only 14 players used by manager Ron Saunders throughout Villa's title-winning campaign but had barely figured throughout 1981-82. When it became clear he would not be in the squad for the final, he had decided to come to the aid of his country.

"I was in South America on a summer tour with the Irish team when Villa beat Bayern," he says. "Even though I wasn't in the Villa squad, I could have gone to Rotterdam with the official party, but the Republic were short of players so I decided to go on the tour.

"I was just sitting down for a meal with the Irish lads when I heard the news. Liam Brady came into the hotel dining room and told me that Villa had won and Peter Withe had scored the goal. I couldn't have been any more delighted and at that moment I wished more than anything I could have been in Holland to savour the occasion. The Villa players when I was at the club were the nicest bunch of lads I've ever met. I was overjoyed for them."

Perhaps the final word of this wonderful story, though, should go to a man who is no longer with us. Tony Barton, who died in 1993, had been Villa's manager for less than four months when they won the European Cup, but he perfectly captured the team's mood when interviewed during the summer following Villa's triumph.

"People have asked me how I felt and the only way I can describe it is that there was a sort of numbness until I stood back and saw how the fans and players were enjoying the occasion," he said. "It was the moment we had all dreamed of. The longer the competition went on, we all believed it was possible to bring the cup to Villa Park."

miss. m. Priestis guest

THE LORD MAYOR OF BIRMINGHAM
COUNCILLOR PETER HOLLINGWORTH J.P.,
requests the pleasure of your company
at a
CHAMPAGNE RECEPTION
in
The Banqueting Suite, Council House, Victoria Square Birmingham
on Friday 28th May, 1982 at 1900 hours
TO MARK THE APPEARANCE OF
ASTON VILLA F.C.
IN THE EUROPEAN CUP FINAL

RSVP

Informal
Admit One

Please show this card on arrival

THE BOYS ARE BACK IN TOWN
The triumphant team arrive back in the UK carrying
a rather unusual item of duty free

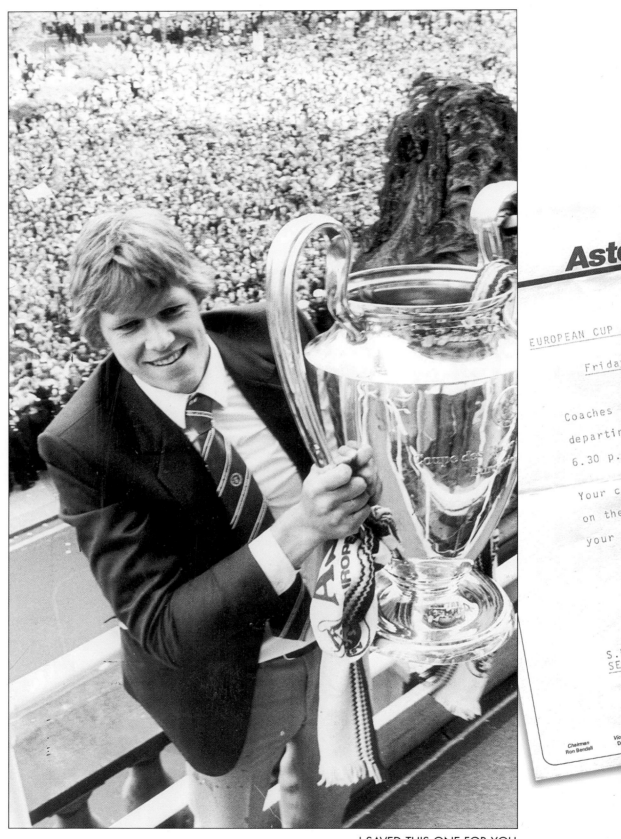

I SAVED THIS ONE FOR YOU
Nigel Spink clutches the European Cup against a backdrop of thousands of cheering fans

KEN McNAUGHT
Born Kirkcaldy, January 11, 1955
Villa appearances: 259. Goals: 13
Full debut: Queens Park Rangers (away), August 20, 1977

"Dad got the caps," says Ken McNaught, "and I got the medals." It was perhaps inevitable that McNaught would become a professional footballer, given that his father Willie was a Scottish international.

Inevitable, too, that he should want to follow in his father's international footsteps, although the closest he got was a suggestion he would be selected for the 1982 World Cup finals in Spain.

That didn't materialise, but the medals certainly did - League Championship, European Cup and Super Cup. There might have been a League Cup winners' medal, too, had McNaught moved to the Midlands just a few months earlier, for he had been in the Everton team beaten by Villa in the 1977 final, a three-match marathon settled by Brian Little's extra-time winner at Old Trafford.

His initial central defensive colleague at Villa Park was Leighton Phillips, but by the start of the 1978-79 campaign he had formed a solid partnership with Allan Evans which was to provide the backbone of the club's domestic and overseas triumphs.

McNaught had turned professional in 1972, making 86 appearances for the Goodison Park club and having the distinction of being Everton's only ever-present during 1976-77.

He repeated the feat for Villa in 1980-81, playing in all 46 league and cup matches, although a knee injury kept him on the sidelines for most of the first half of the following season. He was, however, back in the side in time for the quarter-finals of the European Cup, subsequently playing in every tie. He was once again an almost permanent fixture in 1982-83, missing only one league game, before joining Villa's neighbours West Bromwich Albion for £125,000.

GARY WILLIAMS
Born Wolverhampton, June 17, 1960
Villa appearances: 297 (5 sub). Goals: 2
Full debut: Nottingham Forest (home), September 30, 1978

Injury ruled Gary Williams out of the opening round of Villa's Euro campaign, but having missed the two matches against Valur, he became an integral member of the side in what was effectively his breakthrough season. He had played 21 games during 1978-79, only to be restricted to just one start the following season because of injury problems, although he did have the satisfaction of playing nine times during a loan spell with Walsall and helping the Saddlers to promotion from the old Fourth Division.

Williams was then involved in half the matches during Villa's League Championship season, but it was in 1981-82 that he really came of age in the left-back position, culminating in glory in Rotterdam.

Not that left-back was the only area where he performed competently in claret-and-blue. By the time he signed for Leeds United in the summer of 1987, he had played in over 300 games, displaying his versatility by occupying no fewer than eight different positions.

The move to Elland Road ended a 12-year association with Villa for the former Wolverhampton and Staffordshire schoolboy player, who joined the club as an apprentice in 1975 and turned professional three years later. A substitute appearance against Everton in September 1978 represented his first senior action, and two weeks later he made his full debut in a 2-1 home defeat at the hands of Nottingham Forest.

He looked set to launch an international career early in 1981 when he was selected for the England under-21 side to face the Republic of Ireland, only for a hamstring problem to deny him an opportunity which never presented itself again.

If he missed out on international honours, though, Williams will always be fondly remembered by Villa supporters for his consistent club performances over the best part of a decade.

DES BREMNER
Born Aberchirder, September 7, 1952
Villa appearances: 221(5 sub). Goals: 10
Full debut: Arsenal (home), September 22, 1979

Very much the Mr Versatile of the Euro squad, Des Bremner was essentially a right-sided midfielder whose non-stop running was a key feature of many Villa attacks. He was, however, equally comfortable at full-back or in central defence, which proved invaluable when he stood in for the injured Allan Evans in the quarter-final away leg against Dynamo Kiev.

The hard-working Scot, in fact, had stated his career as a defender with Hibernian, joining the Edinburgh club in 1971 and turning professional the following year. It was during his time at Easter Road that he was converted to a midfielder, scoring 22 goals in 255 games for Hibs before joining Villa in September, 1979 in a £250,000 transfer which saw striker Joe Ward move in the opposite direction.

As a Hibs player, he won nine Scottish under-23 caps, making his only senior appearance as a substitute against Switzerland in 1976. He also picked up runners-up medals in both the Scottish Cup and League Cup, but if he just missed out on major honours north of the border he more than made amends in the Midlands, enjoying triumphs in the League Championship, European Cup and European Super Cup as well as playing in the World Clubs Championship against Penarol in Tokyo.

His playing style and personality epitomised Villa's success in the early eighties. Modest and understated, he simply got on with the job, content to be a vital cog in a smooth-running machine. His Villa Park career came to an end in October, 1984 when he was signed by Ron Saunders for the second time in a transfer which took him to Birmingham City.

DENNIS MORTIMER
Born Liverpool, April 5, 1952
Villa appearances: 403 (1 sub). Goals: 36
Full debut: West Ham (home), December 26, 1975

Jimmy Rimmer and Peter Withe may have been older, but Dennis Mortimer was very much the father figure of the most successful era of Aston Villa's history. The longest-serving member of the European Cup squad, he was also the captain and the undisputed driving force, making great demands on both himself and his colleagues, as well as striking fear into the hearts of opposition defences with his forceful runs from midfield. He was also a seasoned Euro-campaigner, both before and after the pinnacle of 1982. During his time in claret-and-blue, Villa played 28 competitive matches against international opponents, and Mortimer missed only one - the 3-0 second leg Super Cup victory over Barcelona.

Yet it was at another Midland club that Mortimer first came to prominence, moving from his Merseyside home to join Coventry City as an apprentice in 1967.

After turning professional two years later, he made more than 200 appearances for the Sky Blues before signing for Villa for £175,000 in 1975. The deal was concluded on December 23, with Steve Stride - then assistant secretary - having to deliver the transfer forms to the Football League headquarters in Lytham on Christmas Eve in order for Mortimer to make a Boxing Day debut against West Ham.

Having collected a League Cup medal when Villa beat Everton in the marathon final of 1977, Mortimer subsequently had the satisfaction of holding aloft both the League Championship trophy and the European Cup. Yet surprisingly he never played for England, having to be content with Youth, under-23 and B caps. He left Villa to join Brighton and Hove Albion in 1985, and by the time he retired two years later, after a season with Birmingham City, he had amassed more than 700 League and Cup appearances for his various clubs.

GORDON COWANS
Born Durham, October 27, 1958
Villa appearances: 515 (22 sub). Goals: 59
Full debut: Norwich City home (League Cup), September 26,1976

Very much Aston Villa's Prodigal Son, Gordon Cowans returned to the club not once, but twice - and was held in such esteem that he was awarded a testimonial while playing for another club! Popularly known by his second name Sid, Cowans was always destined to wear claret-and-blue, having been on schoolboy forms with Villa since the age of 12, which may explain why he was always tempted back to Villa Park. Although he was born in the North East, his family had moved to Mansfield by the time he was three and it was there that he was spotted by Villa scouts and invited to play for the club's nursery team, Stanley Star.

On leaving school, he graduated through Villa's youth and reserve sides, getting his first taste of senior action at the age of 17, when he went on as a late substitute at Maine Road. His big breakthrough, however, came in September, 1976, when he made his full debut in a 2-1 League Cup win over Norwich City. By the end of that season, he was a first team regular and the proud possessor of a League Cup medal, following Villa's victory over Everton in a marathon final which was decided after extra-time in the second replay.

Between 1979 and 1983, Cowans did not miss a single match during the most successful period of the club's history, picking up further medals for triumphs in the League Championship, European Cup and European Super Cup. Having also won eight England caps as a Villa player, he joined Italian club Bari in 1985, returning three years later when Graham Taylor signed him for the club's return to the top flight. He was sold to Blackburn Rovers in 1991, but returned for a third spell with Villa before joining Derby County.

TONY MORLEY
Born Ormskirk, August 26, 1954
Villa appearances: 169 (10 sub). Goals: 34
Full debut: Bolton Wanderers (away), August 18, 1979

If Peter Withe was Villa's European Cup-winner, most Villa supporters will recall with equal relish Tony Morley's delightful footwork and fine low centre which set up the 67th minute winner in Rotterdam. That flash of flamboyance was typical of a classy winger whose ability to beat defenders and provide accurate crosses made him the scourge of many a defence.

Throw in the ability to score on a fairly regular basis, and you have the complete midfielder. Morley joined Villa from Burnley for £200,000 in the summer of 1979, having previously played for Preston North End, and while he had nurtured his sublime skills in Lancashire, it was during his four years in Birmingham that he became the finished article. An ever-present during the Championship season of 1980-81, he contributed 10 important goals to supplement the Withe-Shaw output, and also had the distinction of being Villa's leading scorer during their Euro campaign.

Although his League return of six goals in 37 appearances was modest by comparison with his exploits of the pervious season, he was deadly against foreign opposition, hitting the target four times in eight matches.

Morley continued to exhibit his talents throughout the following season, playing in both the European Super Cup against Barcelona and the World Clubs Championship against Penarol in Tokyo, but after only half a dozen appearances in the early stages of 1983-84, he was transferred to West Bromwich Albion for £75,000.

Morley served under manager Ron Saunders at three different clubs - Villa, Birmingham City and Albion during a second spell at The Hawthorns. He won six full England caps, as well as representing his country at youth, under-23 and B level.

GARY SHAW
Born Kingshurst, January 21, 1961
Villa appearances: 204 (8 sub). Goals: 80
Full debut: West Bromwich Albion (away), November 25, 1978

Gary Shaw's local roots made him a firm favourite with Holte Enders - particularly as he also formed a potent striking partnership with Peter Withe.

Shaw's pace and anticipation, allied to Withe's power, struck fear into the heart of any opposition defence, providing the finishing touch to a Villa side who were very much a unit rather than a collection of individuals.

Shaw's exploits in foreign fields did, however, set him slightly apart from his team-mates. Having been voted PFA Young Player of the Year in 1981, he went one better the following season, receiving the accolade of European Young Footballer of the Year - an honour which earned him an impressive shield and a three-week holiday in Italy.

The blond-haired boy from Kingshurst began his apprenticeship with Villa in the summer of 1977, and by the end of the following year he had been given his first taste of senior football, going on as a substitute at Bristol City before starting his first match against Villa's Midland rivals West Bromwich Albion.

He signed professional on his 18th birthday, establishing himself a first team regular during the 1979-80 season, and missed only two games throughout Villa's Championship season, during which he scored 18 goals.

Shaw's Euro award followed some outstanding displays en route to Rotterdam, featuring two goals in the first round second leg against Valur and a rather more vital strike for the breakthrough goal in the quarter-final against Dynamo Kiev.

He was also a regular member of the side throughout 1982-83, before a series of injuries disrupted his career. His appearances over the next five years were severely restricted, and he was given a free transfer in 1988.

PETER WITHE
Born Liverpool, August 30, 1951
Villa appearances: 232. Goals: 90
Full debut: Leeds United (away), August 16, 1980

When Peter Withe arrived at Villa Park in the summer of 1980, he was described by manager Ron Saunders as "the last piece in the jigsaw."

Even the astute Saunders, though, could barely have imagined just how snugly the Liverpool-born striker would fit into a compact Villa unit who had promised much the previous season but had settled for seventh in the table largely through their lack of goals.

Withe, a club record signing at £500,000, quickly provided the remedy to that particular problem, scoring 20 league goals as Villa won the title for the first time in 71 years. The following season, his First Division total was halved, but that hardly mattered as he came up with the most important goal in the club's history on that May night in Holland.

But it wasn't just his goalscoring prowess which made him such a popular figure during five years down Witton way. Withe was also a showman and at the end of each home match he ran to the Holte End, where he collected a bag of sweets from one of his adoring fans.

Withe was 29 when he arrived at Villa, having already played for Southport, Barrow, Wolves, Birmingham City, Nottingham Forest and Newcastle United.

He had the option of joining a number of clubs that summer, including his boyhood favourites Everton, but decided Villa offered the best chance of a second Championship medal to add to the one he had won with Forest.

His vision could not have been more accurate, his success in claret-and-blue being mirrored by 11 England caps before, at the age of 34, he joined Sheffield United on a free transfer. He later had a spell as Villa's assistant manager when Jo Venglos was in charge.

DAVID GEDDIS

Born Carlisle, March 12, 1958
Villa appearances: 51 (4 sub). Goals: 16
Full debut: Arsenal (home), September 22, 1979

David Geddis proudly boasts a medal collection which would be the envy of any footballer, collecting mementoes from all three of the most prestigious competitions pursued by English clubs. Having been an FA Cup winner with Ipswich Town in 1978, when he helped the Portman Road club to a Wembley victory over Arsenal, he played eight times and scored four goals during Villa's League Championship season as well as being among the substitutes the night they lifted the European Cup.

Geddis began his career with Ipswich in 1975, turning professional shortly after his 17th birthday and won an England B cap during his time with the Suffolk club. He cost Villa a club record £350,000 when he joined them in September 1979, and played 20 games by the end of that season but never again managed to command a regular place, moving to Barnsley in 1983.

PAT HEARD

Born Hull, March 17, 1960
Villa appearances: 20 (5 sub). Goals: 2
Full debut: Norwich City (home), March 26, 1980

Pat Heard arrived from Everton in October, 1979 as a makeweight in the £650,000 deal which took John Gidman to Goodison Park. He had played a dozen games for Everton as a teenager, although his debut for the Merseysiders never went into the record books. With the score standing at 1-1, the New Year's Day match against Bolton Wanderers was abandoned at half-time because of snow.

Heard was valued at £100,000 as part of the exchange, but his career was put on hold in 1981 when he was out of football for eight months because of a heart problem. Despite making a full recovery, he was unable to command a place in a side who had just won the title, although he was substitute in both the second leg of the European semi-final against Anderlecht and the final.

His only European action for Villa, before he joined Sheffield Wednesday in January,1983 was in the behind-closed doors first round clash against Besiktas at Villa Park.

IVOR LINTON
Born West Bromwich, November 20, 1960
Villa appearances: 17 (11 sub). Goals: 0
Full debut: Bristol City (home) November 18,1978

Despite only being among the "fringe" players in Villa's European squad, Ivor Linton at least saw some action when he went on as substitute for the injured Gary Williams during the 2-1 second round victory away to Dynamo Berlin.
Linton had the misfortune of conceding a penalty in that match when he was somewhat harshly adjudged to have brought down Wolf-Rudiger Netz, but at least it was not a costly error, Artur Ullrich hitting the post from the spot before goalkeeper Jimmy Rimmer saved the rebound.
A utility player, Linton was spotted by Villa scouts when he played for Staffordshire Schoolboys and was invited to the club for trials. He was taken on to the playing staff on his 17th birthday, and made his first senior appearance while still an apprentice when he went on as substitute at home to Stoke City in May,1977. He also had a taste of European football in September that year, replacing John Deehan during the second leg UEFA cup clash away to Turkish club Fenerbahce, which Villa won 2-0. His Villa days came to an end with a move to Peterborough United in 1982.

EAMONN DEACY
Born Galway, October 1, 1958
Villa appearances: 30. Goals: 1
Full debut: Leeds United (away), April 19,1980

Although he didn't kick a single ball during the victorious Euro campaign, Eamonn Deacy already had the distinction of being one of only 14 players used by Villa throughout their League Championship season, starting five matches. The amiable Irishman arrived at Villa Park from his home town club Galway Rovers in March 1979, having spent eight months writing around 20 letters in the hope of being given a trial. He got his first taste of senior involvement in December that year, when he went on as substitute for David Geddis in a 2-1 win over Tottenham Hotspur. After five years with the club, he returned across the Irish Sea in 1984, when he linked up with his former club, who by then had changed their name to Galway United.

MARK JONES
Born Birmingham, October 22,1961
Villa appearances: 28. Goals: 0
Full debut: Coventry City (home), February 27, 1982

Even before he kicked a ball for Villa's senior side, Mark Jones helped the club to win three trophies. In his first two seasons at Villa Park, he collected three winners' medals at youth level, including the coveted FA Youth Cup in 1980.
A product of Warley Boys and West Midlands Boys, Jones joined Villa as an apprentice in July, 1979, turning professional 12 months later.
His initial outing for the first team was against Valladollid during an end-of-season trip to France and Spain following Villa's 1981 title triumph. He was among the substitutes for the European tie against Valur in Iceland, and was also in line for the quarter-final trip to Russia, only to be grounded when he mislaid his passport. He joined Brighton in 1984.

GARY SHELTON
Born Nottingham, March 21,1958
Villa appearances: 26 (1 sub). Goals: 8
Full debut: Wolves (home), August 19, 1978

Midfielder Gary Shelton joined Villa for £60,000 from neighbours Walsall in January, 1978, with the Saddlers receiving a further £20,000 after he had made 15 appearances in claret-and-blue.
He had joined the Fellows Park club straight from school, turning out in 24 games in red and white before his move across the West Midlands.
Despite his excellent goals to games ratio, including a hat-trick against Arsenal in April 1979, Shelton was unable to hold down a regular first team place with Villa, moving to Sheffield Wednesday shortly after he had been on the bench for the first leg of the European Cup quarter-final away to Dynamo Kiev.

TERRY BULLIVANT
Born London, September 23, 1956
Villa appearances: 11(4). Goals: 0
Full debut: Liverpool (home), December 8, 1979

A popular Cockney, Terry Bullivant was unfortunate to join Villa at a time when they were so well served in midfield. Having won an England Youth cap while at Craven Cottage, he cost £220,000 when Ron Saunders signed him from Fulham in November, 1979, but found it difficult to dislodge the likes of Mortimer and Cowans.
At one stage of his Villa career he was out of the first team for 21 months and after just 15 appearances he returned to London in 1982, joining Charlton Athletic in a £90,000 deal.
His medical when joining the Addicks was actually carried out by Villa's Dr David Targett because Charlton's medical officer was away on duty in the Falklands conflict.

MARK KENDALL
Born Nuneaton, December 10, 1961
Villa appearances: 0

The form of Jimmy Rimmer and Nigel Spink meant that goalkeeper Mark Kendall never made Villa's first team line-up, but he completes the 1981-82 Euro squad by virtue of having been among the substitutes in the home leg against Dynamo Berlin when Spink was injured.

Although he never made a senior appearance for the club, he enjoyed plenty of success at youth level, including eight England caps in 1979-80 which culminated in a European Youth Championship medal. He was also in the England squad who reached the semi-finals in the 1979 World Youth Championship in Australia. In his first three seasons at Villa Park, he played in two FA Youth Cup finals and two Southern Junior Floodlit Cup finals.

Men In Charge

Ron Saunders

If Villa's triumph was essentially down to the players, the contribution of those who motivated them should not be underestimated, either. Ron Saunders laid the foundations with the squad who had won the League Championship the previous season, and Tony Barton completed the job after Saunders' departure in February, 1982, steering the club through the quarter-finals and semi-finals before revelling in the glory of Rotterdam.

On reflection, it is incredible that Villa - or any other club, for that matter - should have survived a mid-season managerial resignation and still gone on to win the European Cup. Such was the self-belief among the squad, though, that they took the shock in their stride, refusing to allow Saunders' decision to divert them from the conviction that their name was on the trophy.

Even without the crowning glory of European triumph, Saunders in unquestionably the most successful manager in Villa's history. Appointed as successor to Vic Crowe in the summer of 1974, the former Norwich City boss led the club to promotion to the top flight a year later and enjoyed League Cup triumphs in 1975 and 1977 before masterminding the 1980-81 title success with a squad of just 14 players.

Barton, who had been a playing colleague of Saunders at Portsmouth in the early 1960s, was the perfect right-hand man, providing an understated approach as a contrast to the manager's more abrasive style. His less forceful methods would cost him his job at the end of the 1983-84 season, but there is little doubt that they had a significant bearing on the European Cup victory.

Goalkeeper Nigel Spink has fond memories of both managers. "We had an exceptionally well-balanced side," he says, "and there were always players like David Geddis, Andy Blair and Pat Heard, waiting to step in. It says a lot about Ron Saunders' man management that he was able to keep everybody happy even when they weren't in the side.

"Tony showed a great deal of bravery in keeping the team ticking over after Ron was sacked. It would have been easy for Tony to try and bring in new players, but he made his mark by being brave enough to keep the squad together and allowing them to carry on playing as they had been in the earlier rounds."

Despite the acrimonious nature of his exit, Saunders was gracious enough to salute the team's final victory over Bayern Munich, even though he had to settle for watching the match at home on television rather than directing operations from the touchline in Rotterdam.

Tony Barton

"I always thought Villa would win the European Cup," he said the following day. "I'm absolutely delighted for the players and the supporters. The players have worked so hard to get to this pinnacle. Naturally, I had mixed feelings as I watched."

Skipper Dennis Mortimer insists, however, that he and the other players were too pre-occupied with the task in hand to be distracted by the change of leadership.

"It wasn't a situation which affected us as a team," he says. "Players are always concerned with what they want to do. I was disappointed when Ron went. To leave when he did was a shame because winning the European Cup after leading us to the championship would have been a true testament to his ability as a manager.

"But Tony took it on for him and ensured that everything ran smoothly. The players knew exactly what we had to do, and we just had to make sure we were ready for each game as it came along.

"Some people felt that losing Ron might have had a detrimental effect, but I never thought it would. We had too much experience for that to happen."

European Cup 1981-1982

PRELIMINARY ROUND

St Etienne 1, Dynamo Berlin 1
Dynamo Berlin 2, St Etienne 0
(Berlin won 3-1 on aggregate)

FIRST ROUND

Aston Villa 5, Valur Reykjavic 0
Valur Reykjavic 0, Aston Villa 2
(Villa won 7-0 on aggregate)

Austria Vienna 3, Partizani 1
Partizani 1, Austria Vienna 0
(Vienna won 3-2 on aggregate)

Benfica 3, Omonia Nicosia 0
Omonia Nicosia 0, Benfica 1
(Benfica won 4-0 on aggregate)

Celtic 1, Juventus 0
Juventus 2, Celtic 0
(Juventus won 2-1 on aggregate)

CSKA Sofia 1, Real Sociedad 0
Real Sociedad 0, CSKA Sofia 0
(CSKA won 1-0 on aggregate)

Dynamo Berlin 2, Zurich 0
Zurich 3, Dynamo Berlin 1
(Berlin won on away goals rule)

Dynamo Kiev 2, Trabsonspor 0
Trabsonspor 1, Dynamo Kiev 1
(Kiev won 3-1 on aggregate)

Ferencvaros 3, Banik Ostrava 2
Banik Ostrava 3, Ferencvaros 0
(Banik won 5-3 on aggregate)

Hibernians Malta 1, Red Star Belgrade 2
Red Star Belgrade 8, Hibernians Malta 1
(Red Star won 10-2 on aggregate)

KB Copenhagen 1, Athlone Town 1
Athlone Town 2, KB Cogenhagen 2
(KB won on away goals rule)

OPS Oulu 0, Liverpool 1
Liverpool 7, OPS Oulu 0
(Liverpool won 8-0 on aggregate)

Oesters Vaxjo 0, Bayern Munich 1
Bayern Munich 5, Oesters Vaxjo 0
(Bayern won 6-0 on aggregate)

Progres Niedercorn 1, Glentoran 1
Glentoran 4, Progres Niedercorn 0
(Glentoran won 5-1 on aggregate)

Start Kristiansand 1, AZ Alkmaar 3
AZ Alkmaar 1, Start Kristiansand 0
(AZ won 4-1 on aggregate)

Uni Craiova 3, Olympiakos 0
Olympiakos 2, Uni Craiova 0
(Uni Craiova won 3-2 on aggregate)

Widsew Lodz 1, Anderlecht 4
Anderlech 2, Widsew Lodz 1
(Andelecht won 6-2 on aggregate)

SECOND ROUND

Anderlecht 3, Juventus 1
Juventus 1 Anderlecht 1
(Anderlecht won 4-2 on aggregate)

Austria Vienna 0, Dynamo Kiev 1
Dynamo Kiev 1, Austria Vienna 1
(Kiev won 2-1 on aggregate)

AZ Alkmaar 2, Liverpool 2
Liverpool 3, AZ Alkmaar 2
(Liverpool won 5-4 on aggregate)

Banik Ostrava 3, Red Star Belgrade 1
Red Star Belgrade 3, Banik Ostrava 0
(Red Star won 4-3 on aggregate)

Benfica 0, Bayern Munich 0
Bayern Munich 4, Benfica 1
(Bayern won 4-1 on aggregate)

CSKA Sofia 2, Glentoran 0
Glentoran 2, CSKA Sofia 1
(CSKA won 3-2 on aggregate)

Dynamo Berlin 1, Aston Villa 2
Aston Villa 0, Dynamo Berlin 1
(Villa won on away goals rule)

KB Copenhagen 1, Uni Craiova 0
Uni Craiova 4, KB Copenhagen 1
(Uni Craiova won 4-2 on aggregate)

QUARTER-FINALS

Anderlecht 2, Red Star Belgrade 1
Red Star Belgrade 1, Anderlecht 2
(Anderlecht won 4-2 on aggregate)

Dynamo Kiev 0, Aston Villa 0
Aston Villa 2, Dynamo Kiev 0
(Villa won 2-0 on aggregate)

Liverpool 1, CSKA Sofia 0
CSKA Sofia 2, Liverpool 0
(CSKA won 2-1 on aggregate)

Uni Craiova 0, Bayern Munich 2
Bayern Munich 1, Uni Craiova 1
(Bayern won 3-1 on aggregate)

SEMI-FINALS

Aston Villa 1, Anderlecht 0
Anderlecht 0, Aston Villa 0
(Villa won 1-0 on aggregate)

CSKA Sofia 4, Bayern Munich 3
Bayern Munich 4, CSKA Sofia 0
(Bayern won 7-4 on aggregate)

FINAL (Rotterdam)
Aston Villa 1, Bayern Munich 0